JOCK STEIN
The Authorized Biography

JOCK STEIN

The Authorized Biography

Ken Gallacher

Foreword by Hugh McIlvanney

STANLEY PAUL
London Melbourne Auckland Johannesburg

Stanley Paul and Co. Ltd

An imprint of Century Hutchinson Ltd

Brookmount House, 62–65 Chandos Place
Covent Garden, London WC2N 4NW

Century Hutchinson Australia (Pty) Ltd
PO Box 496, 16–22 Church Street, Hawthorn, Melbourne, Victoria 3122

Century Hutchinson New Zealand Limited
191 Archers Road, PO Box 40–086, Glenfield, Auckland 10

Century Hutchinson South Africa (Pty) Ltd
PO Box 337, Bergvlei 2012, South Africa

First published 1988

Set in Linotron Baskerville by
Input Typesetting Limited, London SW19 8DR

Printed and bound in Great Britain by
Anchor Brendon Ltd, Tiptree, Essex

British Library Cataloguing In Publication Data
Gallacher, Ken
Jock Stein: the authorised biography.
1. Association football. Clubs. Management.
Stein, Jock—Biographies
I. Title
338.7′6179633463′0924

ISBN 0 09 164410 0

Contents

Acknowledgements

The author and publishers would like to thank the following for their permission to reproduce copyright photographs (identified by caption):

AllSport: With Neville Southall
Colorsport: Jimmy Johnstone, Graeme Souness, Pat Crerand, Lawrie McMenemy, At the World Cup draw for the Finals in Spain, David Narey scores for Scotland against Brazil, Steve Archibald tussles with Cerezo
The Daily Record: The triumphant manager, Jock Stein arrives back at Celtic Park, On the beach in Portugal – but not on holiday
The Glasgow Evening Times: Some of the silverware at Celtic Park
The Keystone Collection: Tommy Gemmell equalizes against Inter Milan in the 1967 European Cup final
The London Express: Jock and Jean Stein outside Buckingham Palace
The Scottish Daily Mail: Outside Hampden Park with the Scottish Cup, A proud Jock Stein with daughter Ray on her wedding day
Bob Thomas: SFA secretary Ernie Walker, Jock Stein talks things over with a worried looking Alex Ferguson, Stein on the training ground at a Scotland team work-out

Foreword

by Hugh McIlvanney

Now, so many months after Jock's death, the memories of him that frequently come to mind tend to bring a smile, even an involuntary laugh, which can draw some strange looks if you happen to be alone on the street or in a tube train at the time. Naturally enough, some of my most vivid recollections of him involve footballers he worked with, and none figures more often in those scenes from the past than Jimmy Johnstone, the tiny red-haired outside-right of Celtic and Scotland who probably would have looked more at home in riding silks than in a football shirt. Jimmy was a wonder, a truly inspired winger, whose darting, jinking dribbles could, in Paddy Crerand's often quoted phrase, 'leave defenders with twisted blood'. But, off the field, his antics were liable to be the stuff of which managers' nervous breakdowns are made. Even for Stein he was a handful.

'When I retire maybe I should be remembered not for the honours won but for keeping the wee man in the game half-a-dozen seasons longer than he might have been,' was Jock's considered assessment.

But he acknowledged that the compensations of having such a wayward virtuoso on his strength made the aggravation bearable.

That, however, was never the impression he conveyed to Jimmy.

'Y'know, he's got spies everywhere,' that marvellous little eccentric once told me, staring into my face with his eyes as large as dish aerials. 'He's even got spies in *The Noggin*.'

For a moment, I thought Jimmy was suggesting some infiltration of his mind, a touch of the Manchurian Candidates. Then I latched on to the fact that *The Noggin* was a hostelry, one that the great winger body-swerved into more often than was strictly in the interests of the Celtic training schedule. It turned out that Jock did not have spies in the pub, but had a friend who lived across the way and could observe the comings and goings from his window. Alerted by that watchful informant, Stein would ring *The Noggin* and, in a voice that was gently polite and quite anonymous, ask for Mr Johnstone. When Jimmy reached, unsuspecting, for the receiver he would be blasted several feet by an explosion of the old familiar vituperation. 'Get your arse out of there,' would be the gist of the message.

The relationship between Stein and his star was never easy, but it survived through a long, mutually rewarding run partly because, at the end of the day, brilliance is always likely to respect brilliance, and partly because affection and an element of the comic always threatened to break into their skirmishes.

There were other footballers who did not find Jock's harshness diluted in that way, notably a defender whose reputation as a hard case in and out of football gear was never likely to earn a round of applause. The tough guy was a particular culprit when the Scotland defence disintegrated lamentably against Wales in Swansea a few seasons back, but that did not prevent him from complaining noisily when Stein arranged for a vigorous training session as soon as the party had settled back into their base camp in Ayrshire. He was heard muttering around the place that cancelling the usual day off was out of order. After all, he pointed out in an attempt at the sardonic, even Peter Sutcliffe (the Yorkshire Ripper) was given a day off. Stein heard about the griping and sought out the complainer.

'You've *had* your day off,' he told the player, 'against the Welsh!' The interview and the protest were over.

Sometimes he could amuse without being mordant, such as on the occasion when he picked me up at my mother's home in Kilmarnock and we drove down to Troon at the speed he usually favoured, which meant that only low-flying aircraft were likely to overtake us. We were out to play golf, not at the old course but on adjoining links quite severe enough to tax our limited talents for the game.

When we arrived and stepped out of the car a gusty wind was driving light rain into our faces.

'I think I'll play in the overcoat,' Jock said. 'It won't make a lot of difference.'

He took off the coat, but he did stride out in his street shoes, which scarcely improved a technique whose originality I had previously studied with a shudder of awe on a round shared in Frankfurt during the 1974 World Cup Finals. On that day he devoted so much time to spraying balls and expletives among the timber that his playing companions were inclined to break into a line from an old song: 'I talk to the trees, but they don't listen to me . . .'.

Before all this cheek brings some searing retaliation from whatever Valhalla true Lanarkshire heroes inhabit, I had better acknowledge that at Troon Jock won the money. Trees were no problem there, but I spent more time in the heather than Rob Roy.

'I'm no partner for you,' he said around the sixteenth hole. 'You want that group "The Searchers".'

These last sentences of this foreword are being written in a hotel room in Mexico City a few days after Scotland's miserable exit from the 1986 World Cup. Painful disappointment is a basic and recurring experience for anyone who identifies with Scottish football, but, if the game provides a means for our race to indulge its genius for self-flagellation, it does offer considerable compensations.

It gives us great joyful flourishes on the field – the supreme moments of such players as Baxter and Law, whose peculiar way of being unforgettably great could not possibly be traced to any other ethnic origins – and, perhaps even more vitally, it serves as a language in which some of the most attractive qualities of the Scottish working-class spirit can be expressed. Maybe the old nonsense has occupied too important a place in our lives for too long, but who is going to complain over-vehemently when it has provided such a natural platform for men as appealing and utterly remarkable as Matt Busby, Bill Shankly, Alex Ferguson, and the one none of his peers has ever hesitated to call the 'Big Man'.

Contributors

This book is made up of the memories of the following family and friends of Jock Stein:

Jessie McNeill, Jock's sister, is three years his junior. She lives in the Lanarkshire town where the family grew up.

Margaret McDade, Jock's sister and the youngest member of the Stein family, lives in the same building as her sister Jessie.

Jean Stein was married to Jock in 1946. She shared the triumphs, the disappointments, and the ultimate tragedy over the following thirty-nine years.

George Stein is Jock's only son. He now lives and works in Switzerland with his family.

Ray Stein, Jock's daughter, lives in Glasgow close to her mother, with her son, John.

Sean Fallon, a long-time playing and managerial partner with Jock at Celtic Park, was also a close friend of more than thirty years' standing.

Jimmy Reid is a former trade union leader, journalist and broadcaster. He knew Jock Stein for the last fifteen years of his life.

Tony Queen, a Glasgow bookmaker, was Stein's best friend over a period of around twenty-five years.

Tony McGuinness was Jock's closest confidante over the last years of his life, and was his constant companion to games in England.

Jim Flaherty, better known as 'Flax' to generations of Celtic players, was one of Stein's closest friends. He knew Jock for more than thirty-five years. A familiar figure at Queen Street Station, where he has had his news vendor's pitch for over forty years, he was even more familiar at Celtic Park – and still is.

John Clark started his career in the reserve team at Celtic Park as a very young player. He went on to play a key role in the Lisbon Lions' team, and later he had a coaching job under Stein at Celtic Park. After spells with Aberdeen and Celtic as assistant manager to Billy McNeill, Clark is at the time of writing managing Clyde. He was closest to Stein out of all his former players during the last few years of his life.

Jim Rodger is a freelance sports writer. He was with the *Daily Record* as a staff man when he came into Jock Stein's life. Being a former miner, he shared that special kinship with Stein, as did most miners. He was respected and trusted, and he helped set Jock Stein on the road to his astonishing success as a manager.

Pat Crerand was a Celtic and Manchester United star of the sixties. He joined Celtic as a youngster when Stein was running the reserve team, and then left to go to United, with whom he won a European Cup medal.

George Miller was one of Stein's top players at Dunfermline. He went on to captain the team there, and eventually became manager of the club.

Jim Leishman is manager of Dunfermline. He took them into the Premier League after seeing his own career come to an early end due to injury.

Pat Stanton, one-time captain of Hibs and a former manager of the club, was signed by Stein for Celtic, where he had a short spell as a player.

Jimmy Johnstone, who was one of Celtic's stars in the Stein era, remains a folk hero among the Parkhead supporters. He was one of the great wingers, and Stein used to say that he was better than Stanley Matthews. Frequently, he used to say 'Jinky [Johnstone's nickname] can do things that Matthews could never do.'

Lawrie McMenemy, former manager of Southampton, and then Sunderland, became one of Stein's closest managerial friends. The pair developed the kind of rapport that Stein had experienced with Bill Shankly before the Liverpool manager's death.

Gerry Woolard, Glasgow accountant and sporting personality, looked after Jock's financial affairs for the last fifteen years of his life. He was also a close personal friend and was a man whom Stein trusted totally. He was one of the few men taken into Stein's confidence.

Ernie Walker, Secretary of the Scottish Football Association, worked more closely than anyone else with Stein during his years as international team manager. As well as being colleagues, the men formed a deep friendship, which probably neither of them had believed to be possible when the appointment was first made.

Willie Harkness was President of the Scottish Football Association, and remains Chairman of Queen of the South. When Ally MacLeod handed in his resignation before returning to manage Ayr United a few months after the World Cup Finals in Argentina, Harkness knew whom he wanted for the job – Jock Stein.

Graeme Souness, Rangers' player–boss, was Stein's skipper with Scotland, and they established the kind of rapport which managers and captains need. Now Souness is a manager himself – of Rangers, so long Stein's rivals in Glasgow.

Alex Ferguson, now manager of Manchester United, was assistant manager of Scotland under Jock Stein during his last World Cup campaign.

John Gartland is the son of Jock's daughter, Ray. He is the eldest of Jock and Jean's grandchildren, and he was very close to his grandfather.

Introduction

The last thing I wanted to do when I was asked to take over the writing of a Jock Stein biography was to turn the project into a 'cuttings job'. That is the journalistic term for a piece which is written almost totally from the reading and re-reading of files in any newspaper office.

There were several reasons why I didn't want that, the main one being that Jock Stein deserved more. But also, I wanted to try to get behind the enigmatic presence of Stein which had dominated Scottish soccer for so long.

Hugh McIlvanney had been planning a book with Jock for several years, but their respective work loads meant postponement of the Stein story on several occasions.

When Jock died on that terrible night in Cardiff he and Hugh were making arrangements to spend a week's holiday together to begin putting everything into position for the autobiography. It didn't happen and Hugh suggested to the publishers that I should take over the writing of the book. Once the family had agreed to my doing it I had to decide on the best approach. I discussed this with Hugh and suggested to him that the best method might be adopting the style which has been brought to a fine art by the Chicago broadcaster and journalist Studs Terkel. Hugh agreed.

Terkel carries his tape recorder around with him to produce oral histories on major subjects. His books then tell the stories of major events in the words of people who were involved themselves to a greater or lesser degree. It seems to me that sometimes the voices of the ordinary people who inhabit Terkel's pages, tell it better than all the scholarly tomes you can study.

It's maybe a little presumptuous for me to adopt this style – but it's something I'm sure that Jock Stein would have agreed with. Throughout his life the ordinary working class man or woman meant more to Stein than any list of dignitaries. His solid mining background ensured that.

Even before the advent of Terkel, I had been fascinated by the technique of the interview – or a succession of interviews – being used in this way. Almost thirty years ago two writers in the United States, Nat Hentoff and Nat Shapiro, published a book called 'Hear Me Talkin' To Ya' which told the history of jazz in the words of the musicians who made the music. That was followed by a biographical study of the saxophonist Charlie Parker by Robert Reisner in the same form.

I have tried to follow these examples in writing this book. No one knew Jock Stein better than his family and his close friends. Many may have thought they did, but Stein was a private man, with very private thoughts.

He was also a complex man and therefore you may read in these pages two people talking of the same incident but with a different viewpoint – and both would be equally certain that they knew what Jock himself was thinking at that time.

But, in the end, I hope that I have been able to present a portrait of the man which will give even those who knew him well a better, even deeper, knowledge of the man.

Like everyone who knew him I felt a deep sense of loss when he died. You miss the phone calls at midnight when he would be on a high about something, or would just be wanting to talk about an incident in one of the games involving Scotland.

'When that phone rings late on at night,' Alex Ferguson told me, 'you still think that the Big Man is going to be on the other end.' Fergie summed it up for a lot of us.

I'd like to thank the people who agreed to talk to me

about Jock. Especially I'd like to thank the family who also guided me towards his closest friends and made sure their doors were open for me.

There were occasions when the taping sessions became too emotional, occasions when I wondered if I had asked too many questions. But they wanted the book to be right just as much as I did.

If I can help some of the thousands of people who knew only the public figure know a little more about the private man, about the *real* Jock Stein, then the work has been worthwhile.

1

The early days in Lanarkshire

When Jane Stein gave birth to her first and only son on 5 October 1922, she knew that the boy was set to be something special.

For the boy, to be christened John, was born with a 'lucky cap', an extra flap of skin which Lanarkshire lore maintained brought luck. The midwife assured her that the boy was destined for great things, and Jane Stein never once doubted that.

All through her life she watched the dreams and expectations which had been invested in her son become reality. For John Stein – and he was never anything other than John to her – fulfilled every one of her hopes; and added to the 'lucky cap' legend which still exists among the Lanarkshire people.

Perhaps even without that omen the family from Burnbank would have looked for something extra from the one boy to be born into the family. It would have been a natural reaction for any working-class family to look for the next generation to take the family out of the pit rows and on to better things.

One route used for that was education – but that road was closed to John Stein, who had to go to work to help keep the family.

Another route was through sport. Football or boxing were the natural avenues for youngsters who were hoping to escape from the pits. Stein chose football, just as another Lanarkshire legend, Sir Matt Busby, had done before him.

But, by then, he had become the main provider for his

family after his father had suffered a cerebral haemorrhage as well as several gassing accidents in the pits.

These accidents made Jane Stein reluctant to see her only son follow his father and become a miner. But he did, because he knew that the money for the family could be made underground, and he recognised the powerful bond which held mining families together.

Jock's sisters, Jessie McNeill and Margaret McDade, both younger than him, can remember these days. So can his wife Jean, who first met him when he was a young miner – and a part-time footballer with Albion Rovers.

Jessie McNeill My mother used to talk about him and his 'lucky cap' and how the midwife asked her for that wee bit of skin because it meant good luck both for the baby and for the person who kept it. She had delivered two other babies with that 'lucky cap' and she had these to keep and so she wanted that third, so my mother gave it to her. But she always knew it would bring her baby luck.

Margaret McDade People in Lanarkshire knew that a 'lucky cap' brought good luck, and at one time men going to sea used to try to get a hold of one, as they believed that it would get them safely through any long voyages.

Maybe it did, maybe it didn't – but it brought our John good luck in his life. He was very superstitious, you know, which may have come from that happening when he was born and my mother always talking about it.

Jean Stein We used to always talk of John being born with a 'lucky cap' on his head because things did so often go right for him. He worked hard to get any luck – but he did carry that luck with him for a long, long time.

Jessie My mother never wanted him to go down the pits. That wasn't the life she wanted for her son. My father was gassed several times in the pits, and that added to her worries. Her idea for John was that he should get himself a good trade.

Margaret It was fires in the pits which caused gassing accidents, and my father never enjoyed good health because of what had happened to him underground. It was natural that neither of them wanted John to be a miner – but it was difficult too, for him, to break clear of the pits. Where we lived, everyone was a miner. There wasn't much chance of another life. Not in those days.

Jean When I first met John he was working in the pits, and he was also playing by that time for Albion Rovers. I was about fifteen years old when I met him for the first time, and he was four years older. He was my first serious boyfriend. I met him in Cambuslang – in the chip shop there. He was quiet, you know, just the way our George [their son] is now. George reminds me of how his dad was.

Jessie I can always remember my mother saying that she had wanted John to stay on at school. But he wanted to leave and to start earning money to help the family. My sister had died – she was three years older than John, and she died when she was just coming up for sixteen, and my father wasn't keeping well. When he had a cerebral haemorrhage John became the breadwinner, even though he was still in his teens. He was very aware of wanting to help the family. That's why he left his job at the carpet factory and went into the pits.

Margaret Of course, all his pals were miners. I think there was only the one, Robert Quinn, who played with Celtic for a while too, who wasn't a miner.

They used to all go down to the Miners' Hall where they could play billiards and carpet bowls. On summer nights there were outdoor bowls too. My mother and father were both bowlers, and that's where John started playing. Bowls was one of the few things he did outside of football.

Jessie John was that strong minded that my mother didn't have any option when he decided to go down the pits. As usual, once he had made the decision, there was no changing him. He was just that determined way all his life.

It was a miner he wanted to be, and so he went, without

anyone knowing, to see Mr Porter, an under-manager at the pit. He got the job, and that was the end of the carpet factory.

Margaret Basically he wanted to make better money to help the family. Once he got his start it wasn't long before he was going underground because there was better money there. My father was a roadsman in the pits, and so for a while he worked alongside him.

My mother never stopped worrying about him. John was so big, and, in those days, you had to crawl along to get to the seams. She thought he was always in danger, and it's true that his back was always scratched with him being so big.

Jessie When my father became ill John became the breadwinner – he took that responsibility very seriously. He never let my mother want for anything if he could possibly provide it.

He would be making two or maybe three pounds in the pits, and when he was with the Rovers he was maybe making another thirty bob or so as a part-time player. All the money from his job went into the house. My mother always said how good he was to the family at that time – just as he was all through his life.

To try and balance things we used to spoil him a wee bit, and that meant that he was absolutely handless around the house. He could do nothing for himself.

Margaret Everything was done for him. When he was in the pits he didn't have a lot of time between finishing a shift and then heading off for training with the Rovers. When he arrived home he would be black because there were no pithead baths then. So I would have his shoes cleaned for him and Jessie would have his razor cleaned and ready for him. Mind you, he would always give us some money for doing these wee jobs. He looked after us that way. But he didn't do anything in the house, and I think he was the same when he got married.

Jean Around the house he was completely hopeless, and

he was no help at all. If you asked him to wash the dishes then sure as you like, he would be breaking a plate or a saucer and you would have to take over. And then you would know better than to ask him again.

Jessie He did not like losing at anything – that went way back to when we were young. He could be a right cheat when we were playing cards or anything. He had to win.

Margaret When we were young we used to sit on the floor and play cards. He didn't like sitting up at the table to play because he liked to be able to push cards under the carpet and then win the game.

And then, when the weans were young, he would play them at tennis or something on the back green and he would have his own rules – rules that would have him winning. Really, he was just a big wean himself at heart.

Jessie My mother was always very protective about him. She loved every hair on his head. There was a bit of that about all of us really. We used to get into arguments about him – especially from Rangers fans during all the years he had with Celtic. You know how it can be in Lanarkshire with all the religious differences to take into account.

John was above all of that. He hated bigotry, and even though we were all Protestant there was never any mention of religion in the house. John didn't like it when all the different stories were going about. And they persisted even after he was dead. It was upsetting to the whole family. Even people round about here when he came back from Wales to join Celtic would join in at times. You had to listen to all kinds of stories about him taking private instruction in the Catholic religion so he could join the Church.

Margaret That all started up because you used to have priests going about John's house because he would get them complimentary tickets for the games at Celtic Park. And so, suddenly, all of these visits were supposed to be to give him instruction. It was nonsense. All of it.

Jessie There would be stuff about him breaking the ranks

of the Orange Lodge – and he was never even in that! And stories would go round about how he was beaten up by his brothers because he had gone to Celtic – but he never had any brothers.

Margaret Aye, and it was said that he always played with his sleeves rolled down because he had a tattoo of King Billy on his arm. It was all rubbish. It came from jealousy I suppose, but I don't know why because he never gave anyone any reason for disliking him.

Jessie It's wrong that people should keep bringing up the religious issue because there never was one as far as John was concerned.

For instance, when he was married, Jean was the opposite religion from us. She was Catholic, but I don't ever remember anything being said about that in the house. And I can't remember Jean and John talking about it either. My mother always said that 'as long as people are happy, that's all that matters'. He believed that too.

George Stein The religious business never played any big part in my father's life because, personally, he was never concerned about it. He hated any bigotry on any side. I suppose people made a fuss when he was named as manager of Celtic – there were front-page headlines that he was the 'First Protestant Manager' of the club. That annoyed him.

He kept his own religion and he wouldn't change it because he didn't see any point in all of that. He was born a Protestant and that was that. I doubt if it caused him any worries.

Maybe he was hurt a little when my sister Ray changed her religion and then when I was married in a Catholic Church, but it wasn't a big family issue. He used to kid me about being married in a chapel – but it was just a joke to him. He was never serious about it. If we were happy then that's all that counted with him.

He genuinely didn't like the Celtic–Rangers business, and he didn't like it at all when I was caught up in trouble at school because he was manager of what was seen as a Catholic club. I had to try very hard to stay out of fights at school and all over something which had nothing to do with me. But none of it made him want to alter his own religion. I think that basically he saw all the religious differences in football as stupid.

Ray Stein Dad didn't like all the religious pressures which exist in the west of Scotland. He was able to rise above it all, and I didn't let it worry me, but for George it was hard. He didn't make friends easily at school because of who my dad was. Dad worried about George, but was proud of the way he handled the problems which were not of his own making.

Sean Fallon In all my time with Jock, and in all my dealings with him, I never found him to be in the least bit bigoted. In fact he was more Celtic than Celtic themselves. He lived and breathed that club.

I remember going to Ibrox once to play Rangers and losing the game there to them. Charlie Tully, who could be cruel without realising it because he had a bad tongue on him at times, said we had lost because there were too many Protestants in the team. There was going to be a fight in the dressing room that day and Charlie said to me, 'You're on my side' – but I would have nothing to do with it. But that was Charlie and you had to remember the background that he came from, that Belfast business, you know. But Jock was always above all of that kind of talk.

Jimmy Reid Jock Stein was a man totally without bigotry. There was not a trace of that blight which has scarred the west of Scotland, and football, too, in his make up. In the years under Stein's guidance Celtic came close to being in a position where they were transcending the religious divide which has afflicted football in the west of Scotland. Celtic became a magnet for liberal thinking non-Catholic elements in Scottish life who followed football.

The religious differences have become, for me, a millstone around the necks of the two great Glasgow clubs.

Any advantages, if there were ever truly any at all, have long since disappeared. There are none left . . .

The sheer audacity of Bob Kelly to appoint a Protestant as manager of Celtic plus the attitude of Stein himself did immeasurable good for the club. They were trying to break out of the kind of religious stranglehold they had become embroiled in, and perhaps not enough attention has been paid to this aspect of Stein's managerial career at Parkhead.

Margaret He was really close to my mother and would never have done anything which might have upset her. For instance he never touched a drop of drink in all his life and I'm sure that's because of my mother. She used to say to him: 'If you want to break my heart then just you go down to the pub with your father . . .'

My father liked a wee drink but my mother never wanted 'her John' going to the pub. And he never did!

Jessie Well, maybe there were times when he would go into the pub, but he would never take a drink. He and his pals would go to the pub on a Saturday night, say, but he wouldn't touch the stuff because of what his mother had said to him. He wouldn't disappoint her, you see.

Margaret I'll always remember that if he went out to a party and came in late my mother would say to him: 'You were late last night,' and he would have to tell her where he had been. If it was at one of his pals' houses, Andrew McDade say, she would speak to Mrs McDade just to make sure he was where he had said and that he wasn't drinking. I remember her doing that once and old Mrs McDade telling her: 'Your John was the height of company and he's not like the rest of them. He doesn't need a bottle to keep him happy.' That pleased my mother.

Jessie Even when he was married and away from the house my mother would make ginger wine for him at the New Year. That was his only bottle on Hogmanay – her home-made ginger wine!

Margaret Oh, and she used to make special meals for him

too because his tastes were all very simple and he liked to remember the days he went down the pits and the meals that the miners would look forward to. He loved tripe, totties and tripe, the way the men used to get it in the rows when they had finished their shifts. That and pease brose with a big blob of butter in it. My Peter used to have to take it down to King's Park on a Thursday night for him when they stayed in Southwood Drive.

Thursday night was board meeting night at Celtic Park. Afterwards he'd go home and his mother's tripe would be waiting for him. He loved that – and only his mother could make it for him.

Jean He liked simple things, and he liked to keep up memories of the pits, I think. He used always to say that the miners were the finest people in the world – he felt that after working with them underground. You know, even when he was playing for the Rovers he would come back from the game, if it was local, and head off to the pit to do a Saturday-night shift. I think the manager of the pit was very fond of him and he would give him that chance for extra money.

We were well off then, although young ones now wouldn't be thinking that.

I think by the time we were married he was making about £8 a week playing for Albion Rovers, and then he also had his money from the pits. On a Friday, when he was handing me his wages from the pits, I could have maybe £5 or £6 left from the week before. So you see, we were quite well off. But he was always good to his mother, and to my mother, and they never wanted for anything. We used to do that and we saved too.

Jessie Every single one of us in the family shared in John's success when it came. He helped all of us in one way or another. You just needed to say that you were thinking of getting something, say a new television set or something for the house, and he would walk in with it for you . . .

Margaret That was his delight – giving! When my mother

stayed with me, Jean and him never missed a week coming to see her. They were so good to her and that was his delight.

Jessie It wasn't just our own mother – Jean's mother adored him too. She worshipped the ground he walked on. He shared his success with all of us and he enjoyed being able to help.

Jean He was always close to his mother and his sisters, and his father too when he was alive. They all adored him, my mother included. She thought there was nobody like him. He used to kid the shirt off them, you know, because he was a very funny person. He loved having a bit of fun and a joke with people – with people he knew well. He was very quick in conversation and you wouldn't believe some of the things he would get up to with his own mother and my mother. He had so much patter ready for them whenever we visited, and they loved it all.

Margaret When it was my mother's birthday, John and Jean would come up to see her. Jean would come in with a huge bunch of flowers, and John would come waltzing in behind her singing 'It's My Mother's Birthday Today'. She was important to him – and he was very important to her.

When he went abroad, maybe for some big game, she used to sit in the house and sing 'My Heart is with You Tonight, Son; My Heart is with You Always.' After he took that wee heart attack, the first one all those years ago, she was always frightened for him when he had to go out of the country.

She used to say to him: 'Don't you be taking on a lot of travelling on your own, John. You never know what can happen.' And he used to laugh it off and tell her: 'When I've to sit back in a chair, that'll be me finished.'

He was always on the go, you see. Even as a boy he was never contented. He wouldn't sit still for a minute. If he wasn't at one thing he was at another.

Jessie Even when he was away from here he tried to keep

in touch with the local people. If anyone wanted tickets for big games he would try to see that they got them OK. Or when he was with Celtic he would arrange to get them into the Park to see around the place and all of that. He liked to be able to do that for people round the doors.

Margaret I remember an old man, Mr Hailstanes, who died recently. Well, he used to go down to the Park to see our John and he would get some tickets and maybe a few bob for a drink and then John would drive him home. He was forever doing that kind of thing.

Jessie John was superstitious – that came from his mother. When he was playing football he would come in to see my mother and father before going to the game. When he left and was walking away up the lane from the house my mother would shout after him: 'Don't turn back, but all the best.' She didn't want him to turn back in case that would break his luck.

Margaret Before every big game, a European game, a Rangers–Celtic match, or a Cup Final, I had to get a good luck card from the shops to send to him with a wee green leaf cut off a tree and a wee bit of green-and-white material inside it. My mother had to be sure that he was going to get that card on the Saturday morning. Then Jean had to make sure that John had it in his inside jacket pocket and that it would go with him to the game and into the dug-out at Celtic Park, Hampden, Ibrox, or wherever. She was happy as long as she knew he had got that card.

George He always had little things he kept, like good luck cards he received before games, which always had to go into his inside pocket. Or maybe he would carry a little bit of white heather with him – or little bits of junk he would switch from one suit pocket to another.

I remember once he had a lucky tie, and then he spilled soup down it. My mother couldn't get the stain out of the tie and so that was that – he moved on to some other good luck sign. Most football people have their little superstitions, and he was the same.

Margaret The whole football thing was there in the house when we were all growing up. My father used to be always talking about the football because he had a connection with the Blantyre Vics. John picked up the interest from him.

Sure, after my father had a wee bit of a stroke the Vics' bus used to come by the house to pick him up and take him to the games. Then it dropped him off again near the house so he didn't have far to walk. My mother used to wash the team strips.

Jessie I think my father used to play for the Vics too when he was a young man. And when it came to John starting to play the game seriously he took quite a bit to do with it. What happened was that John was playing for the Barrow works' team and the junior team Burnbank Athletic saw him there and wanted to sign him. It was the first time he'd shown anything at all at the football. In the school team he hadn't been very good.

Anyway, Burnbank Athletic took him away for a trial game and got him to sign a form on the bus which meant he was a Burnbank player. All this happened unbeknown to my father. When he came back from playing the trial game and told my father that he had signed for Burnbank, my father was really angry, and he told him straight out: 'You'll never kick a ball for that team. And if you do go on the park for them then I'll go on the park after you and haul you off again.' He knew how things should be handled by the junior teams at that time because of his connection with the Blantyre Vics, and he thought that they had taken advantage of John. So two of their officials arrived at our house one night. They came to the house in Earnock with a bottle of whisky because they thought they could use that to get round my father. But he just told them: 'You can keep that drink in your pocket and you can tear up the form because my boy will never kick a ball for you.'

Margaret They came on a Monday night, after their committee meeting. They thought they would be able to talk my father round with the drink they brought. John's pal Rab Quinn had warned them that he would never be allowed to play but they thought they knew better. They hadn't offered John a signing-on fee or anything, and my father thought they should have given him the price of a new suit at least. That's how it was all done in the juniors then. He was angry and he was determined that John would not play for them – and he never did. The form was torn up, and the next thing we knew he was playing for the Vics.

Jessie My father used to say to John that any team he played for would need to have clothes poles on the pitch. That's because when he was young John used to play in the rows where the women hung out their washing and John would swing round on the clothes poles when he was playing. They used to play married men against single men for a wee bit of money.

Margaret My mother used to get really annoyed with people when they called him 'Jock'. He was always John to her and to all the family. I used to say to her: 'Don't worry about that. It's just that people know him as Jock.' But she would always answer the same way: 'He was christened John, and that's his name, and that's what he'll always be to me.' And he was.

Jessie It was the football that brought the name Jock. It wasn't in the pits or around Burnbank way. Everyone there at his work or around the doors called him John.

Margaret He never really lost touch with this area. If he found out that anyone round the doors was ill in hospital then he would be up to see them and try to cheer them up. He could always do that right enough. Basically he tried to keep in touch with the people he and the family had known.

Tony Queen He had strong family loyalties and loyalties to his background as well. He had a tough upbringing and he loved his own type of people. What I liked about him was the way he kept in touch with the people from

Burnbank. Maybe because of his job he couldn't do that as often as he would have liked – but he did it as much as he could. Whenever he met anyone from Burnbank he was right back to square one again. He never did lose that touch, that feeling he had for the people he grew up alongside.

You know how some people become snooty and toffee-nosed once they get on a wee bit. No way did that happen with the Big Man. Some guys try to hide their backgrounds. Guys who grew up in Calton or the Garngad but they don't want to have people know that today. He wasn't like that. He was proud of where he came from and proud of the people he had worked with and of the people he knew. And why not? Sometimes people get a few quid and they forget the past. That's not honest. He loved the whole mining thing, and he loved the miners.

Jimmy Reid He had a strong, almost inbred loyalty to the whole Labour movement. I can recall Mick McGahey telling me a story once of the time when he, Mick, was a pit delegate in one of the Lanarkshire pits. There was a strike around 1943 or so. It must have been around that time because there were not many strikes later on because of the war effort. Jock worked at this particular pit, and at the same time he was playing part time for Albion Rovers. In the second week of the strike Jock came up to Mick and pushed some money into his hand. I'm not sure what it was and I don't suppose it matters. It would be two or three pounds, around that figure I would think. Mick asked him what it was and he replied: 'That's what I got playing for the Rovers on Saturday so I'm giving it to the strike fund. I don't feel right that I should have this and the other lads don't have anything.' Mick told him that he didn't have to do this, that there was no obligation, but he insisted. It was an amazing gesture for him to make, and it revealed something of what the man was.

There was a special spirit about him, a real genuine feeling for his mates in the pits. I believe that it continued to the end. I always found him to be supportive, going out of his way to help in either words or deeds.

Tony McGuinness He never changed much over the years in his attitude or outlook. He never forgot his roots. He was working class, he was a miner, and that was always in his mind. He was a socialist at heart and he would never really have been comfortable being anything else. That came from his time in the pits at Burnbank and Blantyre. The story about handing over his wages for a strike fund is typical of the man.

Margaret He cared about people. He used to get upset about all the unemployment which was about in the area because this was still his part of the world, where he grew up. He knew what the miners were like because he had been one and had lived among them all his days, and he never forgot the conditions he had been asked to work in.

Jessie He used to get so angry during that last miners' strike. When he was in his car and driving along the roads and saw all these lorries carrying the coal it used to make him mad because he knew that it was going to beat the miners in the end. He was a miner until the day he died, and that's how he wanted it to be.

2
The move to Wales – and a dramatic return

There was little hint of the glories which were to come in those grim war-time days with Albion Rovers.

To Stein, football was simply a way of augmenting his income. He worked in the pits, he played for the Rovers at the weekend, and he was able to help his family enjoy a more comfortable existence than was possible for some of their Lanarkshire neighbours.

The lure of the game, the obsession with it, came a little later, and it certainly wasn't evident to his wife in those first years of marriage.

It was only as his spell with Albion Rovers grew longer that his love of the game increased. When the move to Llanelli came, and with it the chance of full-time football, Jock Stein realised that this was what he wanted to do more than anything else in life.

Jean Stein I suppose I always knew that football was important to him – but when we were first married it didn't take precedence the way it did later. It wasn't his major passion, if you like.

He had his work in the pits remember, and he was trying to make sure that we had a decent home and a good standard of living, and he wanted to help our folks, too. That was always his main priority. I don't think football was really vitally important to him then. He was with the Rovers when I met him, and through the first four years of our married life, but I never went to watch him, and I can't remember him even wanting me to.

Tony McGuinness The first time I saw him was as a player with Albion Rovers. The Big Man was at centre half on the day that Celtic went to Cliftonhill to play them, and we were lucky to get away from there with a draw that day. He played out of his skin against us – I can remember that.

Even back then he was the man who organised the defence on the field. You could hear him shouting and bawling at the other Rovers defenders. I didn't like it too much then, but I didn't think for a moment how much that ability he had would mean to me and to all the other Celtic supporters.

Tony Queen It's a funny thing but I never did see him at Albion Rovers. At least I can't remember seeing him play there, and I'm sure I would have remembered him because he made an impact on everyone. He was that kind of person on and off the field – once seen, never forgotten!

Jean The one thing at Rovers that used to take him away from football, at times, was the bowls. He used to play round about Hamilton and he won a lot of nice prizes. He was a Lanarkshire champion at one time. But then gradually the football took over and, by the time our Ray was born, it was football, football, football all the time. He used to go to all the junior games round about Burnbank, and when I used to object a wee bit to him being out all the time he used to compromise and take Ray with him. On summer nights, when there seemed to be junior games nearly every night, he would take Ray with him and she would sit up on his shoulders and watch the football. I think it was around then that I began to realise that the football was getting to be the most important thing with him.

Jessie McNeill When the chance came to go to Llanelli, it meant that he was earning his living playing football, and that changed him. He was offered a lot of money to go to

Wales, a lot of money at that time. I think it was about £12 a week, and this was nearly forty years ago. Until then the football had been good, he had enjoyed it, but it was still just a way of making a bit more money to add to what he made in the pits. This offer gave him the chance to play football all the time and it also got him out of the pits – something that our mother had always wanted. She never got over her fears about him being underground.

Margaret McDade I think by the time the offer came from Wales he was ready to play football full time. He wanted to give it a try. My father talked about football in the house all the time because of his involvement with the game, so it wasn't surprising that John took the opportunity to go to Wales.

Jean I know it's been said that there was some kind of row with Albion Rovers and that's why John went to Wales, but I didn't know about that. If it did happen then he didn't discuss it with me. As far as I was concerned he was getting the chance of playing full-time football and he was going to get out of the pits and at the same time be making more money.

When he first went down to Wales Ray and I stayed back at home. I think, looking back, we weren't sure how it was all going to work out, and so we stayed behind. Then after he had been there a little while we moved down. He had been coming home once a month or so, really whenever he could, but the family was apart and that was really no use and so I went down with Ray and we sent her to a wee girls' school there just near where we lived in the town. But after only about eight weeks I had a phone call to say that the house in Hamilton had been broken into. I was in a terrible state, especially as John was away with the team when I got the message. Our Molly [Mrs Stein's sister] phoned to say there had been a break-in. It was a Friday night. I'll never forget that because he had left with the team to go to Hastings where they had a game the next day. He wasn't going to be back until early on the Sunday because it was a fair journey for them to have to go away there.

When he came back, and I remember this so well, I told him about the burglary and said that we had to get back home. Back to Scotland. This was at the end of 1951. I couldn't stay on while worrying about the house we had in Hamilton. It was too much for me.

There was a man called Jack Goldsborough who was the manager then. In fact I think he was just about the whole club himself. He seemed to run everything, old Jack. So that day John went down to the ground to see Jack and to tell him that we all wanted to go home. I told him that he had to do that, you see, and finally he agreed. It meant going back into the pits, but that was just what had to be at that time. He didn't have any idea what was in front of him when we were sitting talking.

When he came back from seeing old Jack, he told me that he was going to go to Celtic. Or, at least, Celtic wanted him. I remember saying that I didn't believe him – and he admitted that he had said the same thing himself when he was told that they wanted to sign him. Because there he was, all those years at the Rovers and nobody had ever come from any of the big clubs. It had to happen when he was down in Wales. And, for us, it happened at exactly the right time. We travelled back to Scotland by train the very next day and there was John going to have signing talks with the Celtic. I don't think he ever realised just how that was going to change his life. All our lives. That was the start of everything really.

Jessie It was a surprise to all of us when the Celtic came in to try to sign him. The break-in at the house had upset Jean, and we knew that he would have to come home. But the way it happened, with Celtic appearing just at that time, was great for him.

Margaret It wasn't just John who couldn't believe that Celtic wanted him. My father could not believe it either. I don't think he believed that John was good enough for a top team. But he was very proud of him, even though, deep down, he was a Rangers supporter. I think he began to realise that John was something special, or rather something extra special.

Jean Actually what he said to me was: 'Sit down, and don't laugh at this, but Celtic want to sign me.' That's how surprised he was. He wasn't carried away at all by being signed because, I think, he kept up with things and he realised that Celtic had a worry over injuries to their defence and he saw himself as just being a stop-gap. I don't think for one minute that he believed any more than that.

The religious question didn't bother him – I don't think he gave that a moment's thought. But maybe his father would have liked, at one time, to see him become a Rangers player. I can well remember when he went up to see his mother and father on a Saturday morning before a game. If they were playing Rangers that day his mother used to wish him good luck as usual. But all his father would say was 'I hope it's a draw' because he was that wee bit Rangers-minded.

Jessie I think it upset John that my father never saw him become manager of Celtic and winning the European Cup and then managing Scotland too. He would have been every bit as proud as my mother was. My father would have enjoyed all of that but he died in 1959. Seeing all that happen would have been his reward from life.

Sean Fallon It's a funny thing, but I couldn't remember Jock from Albion Rovers, and so the first thing I knew about him was when he arrived at the Park after he had signed for the club. What surprised me at first was that he was shown into the reserve-team dressing room. That was probably because we had four or five centre halves on the books at that time already. Jimmy Gribben, the club scout, was the man responsible for bringing Jock back. Old Jimmy remembered him and suggested he should be brought back from Wales.

I think that Willie Toner was there, and Alex Boden

and Jimmy Mallan, so they were all ahead of Jock. I think, honestly, that the chairman, Bob Kelly, saw Jock as being an experienced player to help develop the youth policy at Celtic Park. The chairman was a great believer in rearing your own players, and he wanted someone in there to guide them. But that wasn't at all how it turned out.

Tony McGuinness I don't think any of us among the supporters could possibly have realised the significance of Jock's arrival at the Park. It was a big, big surprise when he was signed, and I think it was all because of Jimmy Gribben who remembered him playing for Albion Rovers. After he was back and he made the first team he was made Player of the Year by the James Kelly Supporters' Club in Blantyre. I can always remember that he got a fridge from the supporters that night; it was the first time I met him, and it was the start of a friendship which lasted until that terrible night in Cardiff.

Jean When we arrived back from Wales he went to the Park the next day to sign and he met Bob Kelly and Jimmy McGrory. There was never much chance that he wouldn't sign with all the worries we had about the house and everything.

He settled in quite quickly, I can remember that. And he was friendly with Bertie Peacock, Bobby Evans and Sean Fallon, of course, and Neilly Mochan. And then there was John Bonnar too, and Bobby Collins – wee Lester he used to call him because he was so small and so they nicknamed him after Lester Piggott.

Sean Fallon It was all a bit of an accident, a freak thing if you like, when he got into that first team. There were injuries and so he was put into the side and he more or less stayed there from that time on. He saw the chance and he took it and it wasn't too long before he was club captain too. That caused him one or two little problems with some of the players who had been there for a long time. Some of them didn't look on him too kindly. He was a kind of 'Johnny come lately' as far as they were concerned.

It's not easy to walk into a club. In any club, well established players can make life difficult for a new boy. I can remember experiencing something like it when I was just a raw player over from Sligo. They used to kid me on about my accent; Bertie Peacock had to be my interpreter because they couldn't understand me at times.

There were one or two of the long-serving players then that you were lucky to get a 'good morning' from. At the time it was annoying, but then you realised what it was all about. Everyone is there for the same reason basically, to make Celtic a better side, a successful side. But there is that selfish thing too – that you want to be in the first team yourself. You are there to prove that you are a better player than someone else, and so there is always the chance of animosity. If you take the place of a player who has been in the team for a long time, then he won't be happy and some of his mates won't be happy. Jock had a bit of that kind of backlash, but he didn't let it worry him. He just got on with the game.

Jean He had good times then at Celtic Park, and I don't know of any problems he might have had – he wasn't one to bring his troubles home with him.

He wasn't there that long when he was made captain, but I think all the players liked him, and even the likes of Charlie Tully and John McPhail, who were the big names in the team, got on well with him. When he was made captain he laughed about it the way he had laughed the day he told me that Celtic wanted to sign him. It was almost as if he couldn't really believe that all of this was happening to him. All those years working in the pits and playing with the Rovers and nothing big happening in his life and then all of this in such a short time.

Sean Fallon John McPhail had been captain, but he had been in and out of the side because of injuries and also weight problems which resulted in him going down to

Tring to a health farm. Because of McPhail's problems the club decided to appoint a new captain, and I was picked for the job. It was a big surprise for me and then I had to name a deputy myself. Now it was a hard decision for me to make because Bertie Peacock was my greatest pal at the club. But I felt there was plenty of time for Bertie because he was that bit younger than Jock and myself. Jock and I were more or less contemporaries, and both of us were coming close to that veteran stage. We were pretty well on.

Anyway it was Jock I picked because I had been so impressed with the way he had handled everything since coming from Wales. Unfortunately my reign wasn't to last long – just one game, and then I broke my arm against Falkirk and Jock took over. That was in 1953, and we had a close relationship from that moment until the day he died.

Tony McGuinness Celtic had been in the doldrums when Jock arrived there. I mean they were really down, winning nothing for years, and then when he arrived there was a bit of success about the place again. He was a born winner, of course, and that rubbed off on other players. I think that Bob Kelly recognised his organisational abilities on the field. He would let other players know what he was thinking during a game and get them to stick to their jobs. You know, a lot of what he did on the field as a player and then later as a manager came down to plain common sense. He would take decisions during a game, and afterwards in hindsight they would look easy. People would say: 'Anybody would have done that . . .' But it wasn't true. At the time, while a game was raging on, he would make the decision, stick by the decision, and follow through with the consequences of that decision. It was a tremendous asset he had.

Sean Fallon Basically I liked the way that he spoke about the game. And I liked the way he went about his training. Quiet. Efficient. Hard working. Also, he had a deep interest in the game. He was always thinking about the game and how we could improve as a team, and he could talk intelligently and sensibly about it. Other players were maybe just thinking about getting away from the Park for a game of snooker, but not him. He had a love for the game and a knowledge of it which impressed me very early on. That's why I saw him as captain material.

Tony Queen At the time he came back from Wales my business was starting to build up and we were advertising in the Celtic programme, and so I used to be there, up at Parkhead. I'd see him at the games and he would kid me on about the odds we were offering against Celtic. He'd always be ready to argue about that with me. When he went into the team he just seemed to take over. None of us knew him – or at least most of us who were going to see Celtic then didn't know anything about him. Just that he had been with Albion Rovers and then in Wales. We didn't expect much when he arrived. We were all to be proved wrong so often down through the years. He was a lot better centre half than people seem to give him credit for nowadays when talk starts about his playing career. I suppose because he was such a marvellous manager his playing has been overshadowed. I liked him as a player. He had great power in the air and a sense of command about him. There were a lot of strong personalities in that team, and yet in he came and took over as centre half and then as captain. There were much bigger names than Jock in the team at that time and yet he won their respect. That tells you a whole lot about the man and about his personality!

Jim Flaherty [better known as *Jimmy Flax*] It was when Jock came back to Celtic that I got to know him. Really I met him through Bobby Evans. He was my china at the time. He had his wee shop just up the street a bit and I used to help him out in all kinds of wee ways and so I got to know him well, and then I got to know all the other Celtic players. Jock was among them.

It was a shock to all of us Celtic supporters when he was signed from Wales – and a bigger shock when he went into the first team. And it was a still bigger shock when he was suddenly the captain as well. It was a fairy story for the Big Man. Like everyone else – and I think the Celtic manager and directors were the same – I thought Jock was there to play in the A team and help the youngsters there. Then Boden and one of the other players were injured, and he was in. He was the first to admit that he was helped by the two wing halves he had with him. There on either side of him were Bobby Evans and Bertie Peacock – you couldn't get much better.

Yet Big Jock didn't look out of place at all. He got in there, settled down and soon he was clearing every ball that came into our box. A lot of them with that big knee of his – that was a little bit of a trademark eventually, the way he would get the ball away with his knee. He was a strong, solid centre half, you know. But even seeing him play well in the team, and knowing that he could handle people the right way, I didn't think he would be captain. I mean Evans was there, and Peacock and others who were bigger names and more experienced. But Jock got the job and he turned out to be a great captain.

Tony McGuinness I think all of us following the team at that time, when he came back as a player, recognised the difference he made to the side. Maybe he wasn't an outstanding individual, some would say he was just a big old-fashioned stopper centre half. But he was more than that, and I think most of the fans could see his influence on the other players in the team.

But one thing is for sure – not one of us saw him coming back as the manager. Not even when he stopped playing and joined the coaching staff.

Jean I didn't see him play for Albion Rovers, but I did go to games at Celtic Park, though I eventually stopped doing that. I was sitting in the stand at one of the games and there was a man behind me, and what he called John!

He left him without a name, just sat there slating him, and I almost turned round and said something – so after that I didn't go back to Celtic Park very much. I always went to Hampden, though, you know, when they were playing in Cup semi-finals or in the final. That was different.

There was a good crowd at the Park, and I remember Neilly Mochan and Bertie Peacock and the likes of them would come up to see us in our house at Whitehill. And at occasions like the Cup Final there was always a special 'do' at Ferrari's, and all the wives would be asked to that. Ferrari's Restaurant in Sauchiehall Street was always the place where Celtic went.

Sean Fallon The game was different then, and maybe that's why Jock stood out. A lot of the players didn't bother about team talks or anything, but Jock did. He thought seriously about the game. I can remember one player sitting reading a book when we were all having a team talk. I thought that was very bad. Jimmy McGrory, the manager, was a gentleman, but at that time managers were different. Players did a lot more for themselves then.

Jimmy McGrory was a very modest man when you consider his achievements in the game – one of the great, great players. But before a game all he would say, most of the time, was something like: 'It's going to be a hard game today, lads.' Then maybe he would tell us to watch this player or that player, and you had to watch them too because there were a lot more personalities about then, a lot more individualism on behalf of the players. Some of them could have won games on their own. A manager then stayed in his office – he never came out on the field with us for training. There was no such thing as a track-suit boss.

Jock, Bertie and myself used to talk a lot about the game. We went to Ferrari's every day for lunch, and afterwards we'd sit there and talk and talk. It was a case of us working things out for ourselves, getting a little pattern of play for that left-hand side of the field, because I was in behind Bertie at left back by then.

Jock settled in quickly, and he settled in well, as the cups and the title we won show you!

3

Success – and the start of a new career

If Jock Stein still found himself unable to believe the transformation in his career, he was in good company. Before he had made the move back to Glasgow, and to the club which was to dominate the remainder of his life, Stein had been known only to the fans of Albion Rovers, to fellow players and to those opposition supporters who remembered the powerful but often raw centre half.

For the first time he had a stage. And how Stein enjoyed that. The years of toiling in the pits before going off to play for the Rovers must have seemed part of another life as he began to mix with the game's greats. Star names were littered through his own team. When he made his debut in a match against St Mirren he lined up between Bobby Evans and Joe Baillie, while in the forward line were Bobby Collins, Jimmy Walsh, Bertie Peacock and John McPhail.

Sean Fallon was at full back, and Charlie Tully was soon to return after a suspension. Before the season ended he had played nineteen games in a decidedly undistinguished season as far as Celtic were concerned. Hibs won the championship and Celtic were left trailing in ninth place – and they were knocked out of the Scottish Cup in a first-round replay with Third Lanark.

It was at the end of the next season that success arrived for Stein and his new team-mates. It came in the Coronation Cup, a trophy which has remained at Celtic Park since that famous victory in 1953. By now Stein was captain, and a year of outstanding success was to follow.

Jimmy Flax I don't think any of us thought that he was going to be a real success as a captain, although there were signs about him that he could lead men. These were the signs which eventually blossomed for him to be a great manager. He could get the best out of people, and that worked for him as a captain too. But the Coronation Cup – we didn't look for anything as good as that. We had won the Scottish Cup in 1951 and that was our lot after the war.

Tony McGuinness There was some antagonism from one or two of the players when he was made captain of the team. Some of that stemmed from the fact that he was a Protestant, but he overcame all the protests by sheer force of personality.

You know, that probably annoyed him at the time because he was so much against bigotry in any shape or form. It used to vex him terribly. Anyhow, he had the ability for the job, he soon showed that. We won the Coronation Cup, then the Scottish League and Cup double the following year. We hadn't had success like that since before the war. It was a good team – or rather there were good players in the side – but Jock helped turn them into the team they were.

Sean Fallon Winning the Coronation Cup was the greatest thing to happen to the club at the time Jock came back as a player. Celtic already had the Empire Exhibition Cup sitting in the board room, and it meant a lot to get the other all-British trophy to go alongside that.

It had come at the end of another disappointing season for us, and no one gave us any chance. Arsenal were the English champions, and we beat them 1–0, and then it was Manchester United, and finally Hibs, who had just lost the Scottish title to Rangers on goal average. On the other hand, we were eighth in the League, had failed to qualify for the League Cup knock-out stages, and had been beaten by Rangers at Ibrox in the Scottish Cup.

But the Coronation Cup tournament, and the victory in the final, made us all believe that we were going places as a team. Jock had a lot to do with that, and it was about that time that his very close friendship with the chairman Bob Kelly began.

Jimmy Reid I honestly believe that the successes Celtic had when Jock was captain of the team didn't come from his outstanding ability as a player. It came much more because of the aura of leadership that he had. Now that's an expression I would never have used in front of him because he would have laughed me to scorn. He was so down to earth about everything, especially if anyone was trying to praise him. He didn't like that. But it surely wasn't just coincidence that he arrived at Celtic Park in the dark days when success must have seemed far far away to the supporters, and then, after his arrival, they were winning trophies. And I'm still speaking about Jock the player here. Within a few years of his return from Wales he was the captain of the team which won the Coronation Cup, and then, in the following season, the League and Cup double.

A great deal of success for the team came from his ability to assume command. He was underestimated as a centre half – all you hear from supporters now for the main part is about how Jock would knee the ball away to safety out of the penalty box. There was more to it than that.

Sean Fallon He was a whole lot better as a player than people seem to remember now, but you have to take into account his stay in the team. It wasn't as if Jock had ten years at the top. He was late in joining up at the Park, and then his ankle injury cut short his career. In all Jock had three full seasons in the first team – but we had the Coronation Cup and the double to show for that time.

He was a tremendous reader of the game, and he knew

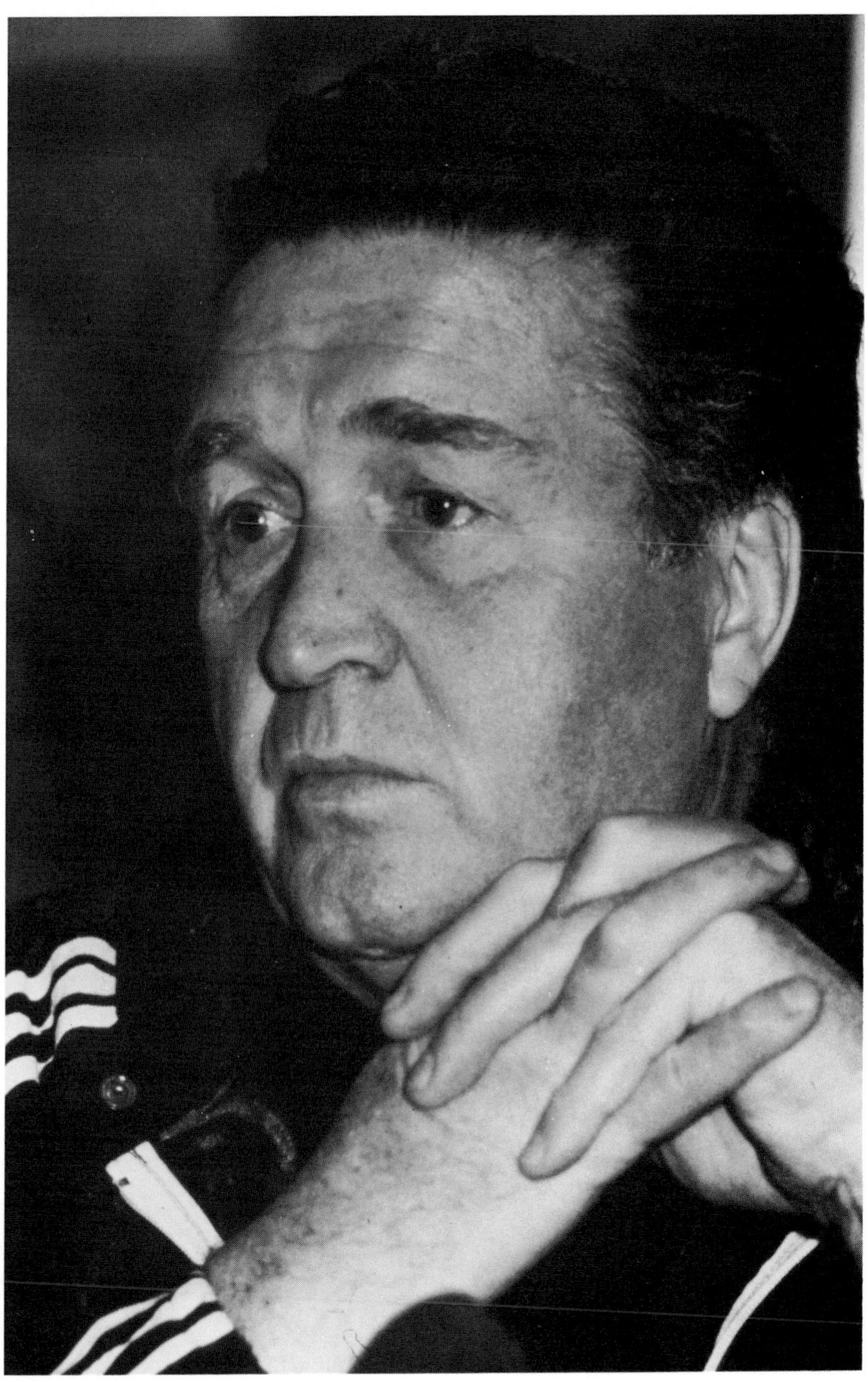

A pensive study of Jock Stein during his days as team manager of Scotland, a rule which covered two World Cup campaigns

A young Jock Stein with his wife Jean

Jock Stein the player, with Albion Rovers

A rare family shot of Jock Stein with his daughter Ray

Man about town in Glasgow, with Celtic team mates, Willie Fernie, the bow-tied Charlie Tully, Bertie Peacock and Alex Rollo

Hampden action from a clash with Clyde and Stein is on the right of the picture with other Celtic players Sean Fallon, on the left, and John McPhail, in the centre

Relaxing the way he liked to – Jock Stein takes to the microphone for a song

The Coronation Cup during the tour of the Supporters' Clubs which brought Jock Stein and the late Sir Robert Kelly so close

Outside Hampden Park with the Scottish Cup and Jock Stein holds the trophy aloft as full backs Frank Meechan and Mike Haughney hoist him on their shoulders. Also in the picture (*left to right*) are Neil Mochan, John Higgins, Charlie Tully, John Bonnar and Bobby Evans

Celtic won the Scottish Cup under Jock Stein's captaincy in 1954. *Back row, left to right*: Alex Dowdells (trainer), Mike Haughney, Frank Meechan, John Bonnar, Bobby Evans, Bertie Peacock and Manager Jimmy McGrory; *front row, left to right*: John Higgins, Willie Fernie, Jock Stein, Sean Fallon, Charlie Tully and Neil Mochan

his limitations – something he was always preaching to young players when he was a coach and a manager: 'Play within your limitations.' He did that himself instinctively. He was good in the air, had a strong left side, and he was always clever and shrewd enough to push opposing players into negative positions – he would deny them any space to play. And then he did have that right knee of his as well.

Tony McGuinness To look back now at those times so many years ago it's almost as if there was a pattern to it all: Jock coming from obscurity in Wales, winning the Coronation Cup and the double, and then eventually becoming the manager. There wasn't any pattern, of course; life is not like that.

But there is no doubt in my mind that Jock Stein's coming to Celtic was the first move towards bringing back the golden days to Celtic. As I've said, no one would have thought that back then. But that's the way it all turned out, isn't it?

Sean Fallon After the Coronation Cup win his friendship with Bob Kelly, the chairman, really blossomed. Jock had always had a great affinity with the chairman. They were both Lanarkshire men, and deep down I believe that Bob always had a lot of time for the miners. They had this kind of understanding, coming from the same area, and after the Coronation Cup had been won, well, they were out almost every night. They were taking that Cup round to Celtic supporters' clubs and miners' welfares and they were just about inseparable. And they had the same interests: football and the horses.

George Stein When I was younger and my dad was still playing, he used to come out into the street to kick the ball around with us. We were staying in the house at Whitehill out Hamilton way and I had friends all round the place. The fact that he played with Celtic, or later that he coached Celtic, didn't mean too much. It didn't make him any kind of celebrity or anything. Not where we lived. He would always take part in the street games, especially on a Friday night. He encouraged me to play, but I don't think that he ever wanted me to be a professional footballer. All he really wanted was that I should be able to handle myself properly.

I think that maybe because I was his son he thought that I should at least be able to kick the ball about properly. He wanted me to be able to hold my own in the games in the street where we played every night of the week, I think, but that was about all. He didn't have any further ambitions for me in that direction.

Still, I can always remember when I was just wee, maybe about four years old, that he took me out and made me kick a real leather ball with my left foot. Somehow, and I can never forget this, I couldn't do it to start off. It was as if I believed that if I kicked that ball with my left foot then my foot would break or something. He stayed there with me until I could do it. Maybe an hour or more just coaxing me to kick that ball with my left foot against the wall. He waited until I had the confidence to practise on my own. That was the kind of patience he would show when he thought we needed time spent on us.

Jessie McNeill There was never a game which involved him that the whole family didn't get uptight about. That was when he was a player with Celtic, and then right through from there. It was him we followed really, I suppose.

Jean Stein I said earlier that he couldn't believe Celtic had come in for him when we were down in Wales. And then there he was the Celtic captain. Again John just could not take it all in really, so you can imagine how he was about the Coronation Cup. And then there was the double after that. He was very proud about helping Celtic to win these trophies – but maybe the Coronation Cup was the most important to him because the club kept that trophy and it was the first honour he had won. He used always to call it Mochan's Cup, because Neilly had just come to the Park around then and he scored the goals that helped them win it.

Tony McGuinness Probably his close friendship with Neilly Mochan came from the successes they shared. He always made a lot of Neilly's Coronation Cup contribution. He came back from Middlesbrough for something like £8000 just a few days before the first match against the Arsenal. He didn't score then, but he scored in the semi-final against Manchester United and, again, in the final against Hibs. The Big Man used to hold up that trophy in the board room and say 'Here it is – Mochan's Cup.'

Jimmy Flax Even as a player he knew everything that was going on. He would be able to find out about everyone in the game, and in doing that he would be able to recognise their problems and their limitations. He knew what every man in the team could do, and never asked them for more.

No one could ever kid him on. Wee Bobby Collins used to say: 'When that big fox goes into the woods all the other foxes run out.' That was his way of saying that the Big Man was ahead of everyone else. That all started when he was a player, and later on it was to help make him the best manager there's ever been.

Sean Fallon When the injury arrived and forced him out of the game I don't think he really knew what would happen to him until the chairman offered him the job as coach to the younger players at the Park. It was funny that should happen because in one sense it was why Celtic had brought him back in the first place. The original idea was that Jock should play in the reserves and help the younger players by passing on his experience.

Jean It was a fairly simple injury as far as I know. John didn't think anything about it when it first happened. It was just a chipped bone in his ankle, but then, when he had the operation for that original injury, something went wrong. It was supposed to be just a routine thing which lots of other players had all the time. But the ankle turned septic – I think it was dirty stitches – and eventually that led to the stiffening of the joints, and that's why he had a limp for the rest of his life. That never left him – though it became worse after that same ankle was damaged again in the car crash.

The injury stopped him playing and so he went on to the coaching of all the young players there: Paddy Crerand, Billy McNeill, Bobby Murdoch, John Clark and all the rest of them. He loved those young boys.

Tony McGuinness It was then that the foundations of the real glory days of Celtic were laid. The youth scheme was in operation – the Kelly Kids the players were called because the chairman had decided to raise the club's own talent as much as possible. And the Big Man's influence was felt for the first time with these boys who were starting off their careers in the reserve team.

John Clark Jock Stein was the start of my entire career in football. It really does go that far back for me because when I went to Celtic for the first time it was Jock Stein who signed me. I signed the forms in the old gym at the Park, and I was put on wages of a fiver a week. He put me on to the ground staff, and I think I might well have been the first ground-staff boy ever in Scotland. From then on everything I did in the game stemmed from Jock Stein and the fact that he was the man who signed me when he was beginning as coach of the reserve team.

I was from Lanarkshire, of course, just as he was, and so it used to be the routine that three of us, Jim Conway, Billy McNeill and myself, would all get a lift back home from him after training at nights. He used to take us in his old car, I think it was a Hillman he had then. We used to stop and have fish suppers on the way home. Before he had the car we all walked up to Parkhead Cross to get the bus together. There was a strong bond between us.

Sean Fallon He made these young players think and talk about the game. And I can remember in those first, early days as a coach he told me something that has stayed with me ever since. He told me that if a player made a mistake in a certain situation and you pointed it out to him, and the following week he was caught in the same position and remembered what he'd been told, then that was a youngster with chances. But if he repeated the mistake, then you had a problem on your hands.

It was one of the little things that he used to pick up on so often and so well. It was when you put together all the little points he would make that you realised all that went into making him such a good coach and then latterly such a brilliant manager.

John Clark His greatest strength was that he would keep the game simple. I can never once remember him using any of the coaching jargon that you hear from other managers. I think some of them use all these fancy phrases to try to impress – mostly they just confuse the players. Jock Stein never did that. You always knew what he wanted you to do. And he would never ask anyone to do anything that might be beyond him. But he could stir people up too, and always it was for the same reason – he wanted to make sure that you were reaching your full potential. He didn't have time for anyone who tried to cheat him or cheat the other players in the team. That really angered him.

Sean Fallon Jock had a way of communicating with players, and I benefited from that myself. I had been brought up over in Ireland, in Sligo actually, playing Gaelic football, and my grounding in football came from my father. All he did was talk to me about the great Scottish teams and players because during the Great War he had convalesced in Scotland and as far as he was concerned Scotland had all the great passers of the ball and all the great individualists and so I was always worried that I would not be good enough. My main aim was to be one hundred per cent fit, fitter than anyone else if possible, and to make up for any deficiencies in my game that way. The other things I had to learn, and while Jock was younger than me, he helped me a whole lot. He could impart his own knowledge, and I found that out for myself, even before he went to work with the young players in the reserves.

Ray Stein Obviously I don't remember too much about my dad having to give up the playing side of the game. But I do know he was always happy coaching young players. He liked that back then and in his managerial times with Dunfermline, Hibs and Celtic. He wanted to help youngsters do well on the field and help them to have good stable lives off the field too. He was always happy when one of the young players was getting married. He believed that helped them settle down and mature.

It was only at the end when he was with Scotland that he found it harder to understand the younger players. By then there was a big, big generation gap, and for the first time he wasn't able to bridge it the way he had always been able to do in the past. That was a problem for him when he took on the Scotland job.

Jean When the chance came up for John to go to Dunfermline he spoke to the Celtic chairman Bob Kelly about it. He did want to go out on his own, but he felt a bond with Celtic and with the chairman and so he talked the move over.

He was more or less told by the chairman that he had gone as far as he could ever go with Celtic – coaching the second team, I mean – and that therefore he should take the chance of the Dunfermline job. I know the old chairman used to suggest that he had simply let John go out for experience and that it was always the case that he would go back to Celtic, but I don't think that was right. John didn't think so either. He thought that Sean Fallon was going to be the next Celtic manager. And he wanted to be a manager himself by this time and nothing was going to stop him.

So that's why he took the chance of Dunfermline. I think he thought that the fact that he was a Protestant meant that he would never be manager of Celtic. That's why he made up his mind to try elsewhere.

Sean Fallon You know he was sad about leaving Celtic at that time. He liked the club, loved the club in fact. He was more Celtic-minded than anyone. He lived and breathed the club even back then.

He felt himself that he had gone as far as he could go with the club. I remember he spoke to me in the dressing room the day he was leaving. He had got a letter from Celtic saying that he could go, and maybe he was a little bit surprised that they were willing to release him without any kind of fight at all.

By this time I was coach, and I think he felt that I was earmarked for the job as manager of the club. I wouldn't be honest if I didn't say that I think a whole lot of people felt the same way. Personally I hadn't considered the situation because I didn't think I was equipped for the job. In any case there was a manager at the club, Jimmy McGrory, a man both Jock and I respected, and we would not have done a thing to upset him in the slightest way. But I do believe that Jock looked at the position at the Park and decided that he would have to go and try elsewhere if he wanted to be a manager. He thought I would block his progress with Celtic and so, even though he might not have wanted to leave, he went to Dunfermline, who were ready to give him his chance as a manager.

Jimmy Flax I can remember him coming into the station to tell me that he had the chance of going to Dunfermline. It was wee Jim Rodger, the sports writer, who got him the chance of the job. I was with him in his car the day he went away, a wee black Ford Popular he had, and I thought that it was all over. I couldn't see him coming back, and I don't think Jock could see it either. All the talk about it being all planned that he would go back to Celtic as manager is rubbish. That kind of talk still seems to hang around the Park, and it's not true. It all grew into a kind of a legend that the chairman took him out onto the field and that, as they walked round the track, he was told that he was just going away to learn his trade as a manager. It's not true.

He thought that was him finished at the Park and most of us thought the same. I never believed he would be back.

Jim Rodger I still have the letter in my house which the Dunfermline board sent to me. Their chairman, Davie Thomson, had two candidates for the job. There was Danny McLennan, who I think may have been at East Fife then. Anyway, Danny was the man with all the coaching certificates – and in later years he went on to coach all kinds of teams in the Middle East and the Far East. Jock didn't have a single certificate, but his work with the young players at Celtic Park hadn't gone unnoticed.

I approached Jock about the job, and it was simply a case that he wanted to be a manager in his own right. He didn't see any furtherance for himself at Celtic Park, and Dunfermline, although they were threatened with relegation at the time, were ready to give him the chance. The day he went through for the interview he had lunch with me in the old Buchanan Hotel in Glasgow. He told me then how much he wanted the job, and I spelled it out to him that it was his already. The directors just wanted to meet him before making a formal offer. He was excited about the prospect, like a kid really.

John Clark I can always remember a kind of let-down feeling when he left. I think most of the players who had been, or were still, in the reserves wanted him to stay, but he felt that he had to make a move at that time and it was a good chance for him. I can remember that one of the first things he did when he took over at Dunfermline was to try to sign me. I was just on the fringes of the first team then. I was kind of in and out of the side – mainly out if I remember right. Big Jock had taken a look at the players he had and he decided I might strengthen the team and so he moved in for me. I would have been guaranteed first-team football and I would have been with him, but it all came to nothing. Celtic didn't accept any offer from him and I stayed where I was. In the end it was a lucky break for me because five years later he was back as Celtic manager and I was still there, but I was an established first-team player by this stage of my career.

Jean It was a funny move for us in a lot of ways. I always felt that John's heart was still at Celtic Park – though he wanted to beat them when they played each other – but he had to move. He was so desperate to try things on his own by this time. It was a wrench for us having to leave Hamilton and all our friends and family, but I realised that it was a wrench for him as well leaving the Park.

But going to Dunfermline seemed like a move to the ends of the earth. I don't think I'd ever been there before. It wasn't so far away, I suppose, but it just seemed that way to me back then. However, we moved into a club house, and the directors and their wives were so good that we soon settled down. The worries I had to start with soon disappeared. That was a happy time for us as a family.

Jimmy Flax I remember going up there for his first game – because Dunfermline were playing Celtic and the Big Man needed every point he could get to keep the club away from relegation. He asked me to take George to the match that day, and there I was with George and he had a black-and-white scarf on already.

Dunfermline beat the Celtic 3–2 that day. Afterwards I was in the foyer of the ground with George and I can always remember Bob Kelly saying to Jock: 'These two points still won't do you any good.' But he was wrong. The Big Man kept them up, and the next season he won the Scottish Cup. He was on the road by then.

Tony McGuinness We – the Celtic supporters, I mean – all thought we had lost him for good. When he left it looked like the end of things. Even when there were broad hints in the press that he was just going to pick up experience, none of us believed that. After all, there had never been a non-Catholic manager of the club and I think most people saw that as being one of the barriers to the Big Man ever returning. He started to show at Dunfermline what so many of us had recognised already – that he was an outstanding motivator of players!

4

Apprenticeship in the provinces

Stein's first spell as a manager was with Dunfermline, and soon he transformed the little Fife club into a team which was feared in Scotland and respected in Europe.

It was a Scottish Cup win over his old club Celtic which gave Jock Stein his first success as a manager. Then he moved on to Hibs before returning to Parkhead.

Pat Crerand I can remember Jock talking to me before he left Celtic, and what he told me disillusioned me a little bit about the club. He didn't leave just to get experience and then go back. That's not the way he told it to me. It seemed that there was no way that he was going to be promoted at Celtic Park and one of the reasons was that he was a Protestant. I felt sad about that.

I knew how well he had done with the reserves. I had first met him when I joined the club from Duntocher Hibs, and he was tremendous. His knowledge of the game, the way he talked about it, meant that we were getting a real education. I was really sick when he left, but I knew that he would be successful with Dunfermline.

George Miller We had never known anything like him as a manager. He transformed the club and he revitalised the whole of Fife. I was one of the players close to him, coming from Lanarkshire.

I don't think we knew what to expect when he first arrived. We knew about him as a player and we knew he had been running the reserves at Celtic Park but we didn't know whether he would be a good manager or not. We soon found out. Within a year we had won the Scottish Cup.

Jean Stein They were happy times at Dunfermline. The board of directors were so good. David Thomson was the chairman, and there was Leonard Jack, Bob Torry and Jimmy McConville, and John got on with all of them. He was fond of the players too – Geordie Miller, Harry Melrose, George Peebles and the rest of them. I enjoyed my time there.

Ray Stein I really became a Dunfermline supporter then. I didn't want my dad ever to leave. I can remember going through to the final to see them win the Cup. My dad had told me I wasn't to go, but I got there with a friend and managed to get a lift home. I can still see my dad at the end jumping from the dug-out with his white raincoat on.

It was all so new and all so nice and all so friendly, and, of course, it was great for my dad to be doing his own thing as a manager. Winning the Cup meant so much to that club and to the whole town really. I loved it. Even when we moved to Edinburgh and he was manager of Hibs I used to go back to Dunfermline to see the games.

Jean There is nothing bad I could say about our time at Dunfermline. It helped that the club had success but really everyone went out of their way just to make us feel at home. That's when I started to go to the football regularly because we used to go to the away games on the team bus too. I even went to Valencia with the directors' wives for one of the European games. It was a great time and Dunfermline was a great place for John to start out. He enjoyed it there.

George Miller It was when he was with Dunfermline that he went to Italy with Willie Waddell to study Helenio Herrera's training methods. When he came back we used to use some of the things he had picked up over there. For instance, I think we were the first Scottish team to use a 'sweeper'. He had Willie Cunningham play that role, and he had me play it sometimes too. And he also introduced attacking full backs. Cammy Fraser, who went on to Aston Villa, was the first attacking full back in Britain. That was typical of the Big Man. He was so far ahead of any other managers in Scotland at that time.

These things may sound old hat now, but they had never been seen before. But it wasn't only the tactics, it was his knowledge of the players. He would never ask anyone to do a job unless he was sure that he would be capable of doing it. He got to know everything about us. He would know which players liked golf, which ones went to the dogs or the horses, and he would kid and joke about it. He would get to know all about your families and he would take a genuine interest in all of us. It was one big family for him.

You know we still get together once every year, or maybe every couple of years, and it's because of the bond that he instilled in us. He had all of us working for each other, and it got to the stage where we were not frightened of going anywhere to get a result. He didn't talk too much about the opposition, he liked to build up your own confidence and dwell on your strengths. He made Dunfermline a big club. I can remember him having us all kitted out in blazers, flannels and club ties. We felt big-time – and that's what he wanted us to feel. He was a revelation.

When I became a manager myself he was a big help to me. But by then the club was on the way down again, and it was hard to pick up the way he had done. It didn't surprise me one bit that he went on to such success with Celtic. It was a blow when he left but I think we all realised that he would move on. A small club could never have held him. But when he did go it was a blow because we thought that we were a bigger team than Hibs! That is the way he had educated us to think.

Jean Just out of the blue one night he came home and told me that he was going to resign from the manager's job at Dunfermline. He could be impulsive in that way, but this time I thought he was kidding because he didn't have another job lined up or anything. I started to laugh, but he told me he was serious, and when I said to him that he didn't have a job he told me not to worry, that something would turn up. I don't know what he was thinking about; even now I find myself wondering about that. I was in a terrible state because we were in a club house and we had settled in well and I thought everything was fine for a few years at least. I think it was the Monday night at a board meeting he resigned, but it didn't come out for a couple of days. I think it was in the *Citizen* on the Wednesday night, and that was the first people knew about it. Twenty-four hours later Harry Swan of Hibs phoned, and on the Friday John went over to South Queensferry to meet Harry Swan and Bill Harrower. And that was how he left Dunfermline. I know the club were disappointed, but they realised the job he had done for them. He put them on the map.

Jim Leishman Jock Stein's chair is still in my office to this day. I won't sit in it, but I would never let anyone throw it out. It is important for this club to remember all that Jock Stein did here. That chair is something of a symbol if you like.

Pat Stanton I don't think we knew what he was going to be like. We all saw what he had achieved at Dunfermline and so we realised that he was something special. But Hibs had been in the doldrums and we all wondered if he could change that. It was a bad time for Hibs – and yet he turned that round.

He looked around for a little while at how things were being handled at the club. Then when he got the feel of the place he started to make changes. It wasn't very long before he had us confident about our own ability. We would go to Ibrox and win 4–2, and we would not worry about who we were playing. He could just give you this lift. He was a great man for taking you to one side. He would have a bit of a team talk and then he would pull you aside and have a word in your ear. It would never be anything complicated, just a bit of common sense.

Once when I was not long in the team he warned me about a little trick Willie Wallace had of coming across a defender and getting the ball to his good foot and leaving you trying to cope with your bad foot. He warned me right before a derby game with Hearts, and sure enough Willie did exactly what the Big Man said he would do. I was too late to pick up on it, and I remember saying to myself 'That's what Big Jock told me to watch.' But it was too late, and Willie scored with that shot. But the next time I remembered.

He bought me from Hibs towards the end of my career but earlier he had told people that, if he had taken the Manchester United job, then he was going to buy me and take me to Old Trafford. I wish that had happened.

When he was with us we won the Summer Cup, and when he left we were in the Scottish Cup semi-final. If he had stayed with us we would have won the Cup that year. Instead he went to Celtic and they were the team to win the trophy. That set him off on that run of success. It was a blow to all of us when he left, but it was too much to hope for that he would stay when Celtic came for him. I still wish though that he had held on until the end of the season. But maybe that was out of his hands.

Jean He liked Hibs, and players like Pat Stanton and Joe Davis, and the chairman Bill Harrower was so good to John. Bill gave him a watch when he left. He wanted him to stay so badly, but when Celtic made him the offer that was that.

Pat Crerand When I was told Jock was going back to Celtic I was so pleased for him. I knew that was what he wanted. I told someone then that he would win the championship for the next six years. I was wrong – he won it nine times. He went on to make Celtic what they are. They should rename the ground: it should be called Stein Stadium.

5
Back home – to glory!

At the time the offer to return to Celtic arrived in March 1965, Stein had built up a close friendship with his Easter Road chairman Bill Harrower.

It was to be a wrench for him to leave Hibs. But the lure of that Parkhead return, a homecoming in so many ways, was too much for even as determined a realist as Stein. There is little doubt that the overwhelming sentiment he felt for Celtic influenced him, but he was not blinded to the problems which might lie ahead.

He knew he was leaving a club which he had been building just as successfully as he had built Dunfermline in his first job. The pressures to do the same at Celtic would be immense.

But then, Celtic had brought him back from Llanelli; surely he had a debt to repay. That is the way his mind worked when the call came.

Neither he nor any of his closest friends, nor his immediate family, went along with the cosy theory that he had been sent out to learn his trade, and that he was always destined to return. It had not been that way when he left. He had gone to find out for himself whether he could become a good manager. Now he was returning to see if he could become a great manager.

But Jock Stein was in charge of his own destiny. No promises had been made to him. Probably none had been expected by the strong-willed Stein whose independence had been strengthened by his years in the pits – and by his years in the soccer shadows before Celtic eventually gave him a platform for that quality of leadership they now needed again.

Jean Stein When the word came from Celtic that they wanted him to go back there, he was delighted. We all were. He thought that it was a marvellous thing for him to be going back there as the manager because he had never thought he would get the job.

The only upsetting thing was that he had to leave a good crowd of players at Hibs and also the chairman there, Bill Harrower. He had been close to John, and when John first told him that he had the chance to go to Celtic Bill Harrower tried to persuade him to stay.

If the truth be told, Bill Harrower came to me as well and asked me to use my influence with John. He thought I could get him to change his mind and stay. But I had to tell him that I could not do that. This was a dream for John, to go back as the manager of Celtic. And even the good times he had had with Hibs, and was still having with them, couldn't alter the fact that he had to go back to the Park. He was surprised when the call came because he always thought that Sean Fallon would have been made manager.

Sean Fallon I wasn't actually assistant manager at the time. I was coach really, I suppose, and certainly I was there with the first team working with Mr McGrory. Anyhow the chairman, Bob Kelly, called me in one day and told me that he was bringing Jock back as the manager and he thought that I should go over to Easter Road and talk things out with Jock.

Hibs were playing Aberdeen that night, and I went through to Edinburgh early in the day and went to have a cup of tea with Jock. We sat and discussed things, and he told me then that what he wanted to impress on me was that I didn't have to worry over my position at Celtic.

The way he put it, he said, this is just an old partnership being renewed.

I think he felt upset in case I was worrying over what my own future was going to be. He said that he wanted to lay any kind of problem at rest immediately because his return wasn't going to make all that much difference to me. I can still remember him saying how funny it was that I had asked him to be my vice captain with Celtic – and that led him to the captaincy – and now here the positions were reversed and I was going to be his number two.

Funnily enough there was a story within a story that night because we were trying to sign Davie Hay from Paisley Boys' Guild, and at the game Jock mentioned that he had heard that Tommy Docherty was up in Edinburgh to see the player and take him down to Chelsea. So I left before the game was over, went to the North British Hotel and met up with Davie Hay and his father there. I took them both back to Glasgow with me. I missed most of that match – but I did get Davie Hay!

Tony McGuinness I thought that when he came back the club had chances of re-establishing itself in the forefront of the Scottish game once more. I didn't dare dream of any more than that. What happened in those first few years was unbelievable. He founded the modern Celtic.

Just to win a trophy on the home scene would have been an achievement. Doing what he did changed the whole face of the game in Scotland.

Jimmy Flax I used to run a supporters' club, and no one wanted to know about the Celtic. I had three boys of my own and they wouldn't go and watch them because Celtic couldn't win a game. Then Jock came back and they went to the games and they are still going to the games home and away. That was my boys, and the story must have been repeated thousands of times over. He ended the black days, and they had been *black* days. People shouldn't forget the state the club was in when the Big Man took over. And from then on it was success, success, success. . . .

I've heard some people suggest other managers could have done the same. I've never known of any, nor heard of any, who could have come near him.

Jean Leaving Bill Harrower did worry John because Mr Harrower was such a nice person. He was a gentleman, and he thought the world of John.

But once the chance came to go back to Celtic that was it as far as Hibs were concerned. As well as going back to the club, he was going back to so many of the young players who had been in the reserves when he was running the second team. They were in the first team by this time, and he thought it would be good to get back and to be working with so many of them once again. It had upset him to see Celtic doing badly, though when he played them with Dunfermline or Hibs he wanted to win. But generally he didn't like to see Celtic in trouble.

Tony McGuinness It was astonishing that he should be there only six weeks and win the Scottish Cup. That was the first time Celtic had been able to win the Scottish Cup since he had been captain. After that double year they had the League Cup in 1957 and not another thing to shout about until he came back as the manager.

That win set Celtic off on the glory run they had while he was their manager. When Billy McNeill scored the goal which beat Dunfermline, the Stein era of success was under way.

Sean Fallon There was a whole lot of fuss made at the time about Jock being the first Protestant manager that Celtic had ever had. But it didn't upset any of us. It annoyed Jock on the day one of the newspapers carried that as their front-page story – but it didn't worry him for long. And it wasn't a problem for the chairman either. Bob Kelly didn't care about the religious issue, and his respect for Jock was boundless.

The relationship which built up between the two men was important to what happened with Celtic. They got on very well, and Bob was there every day of the week. He would be there to see the training in the mornings and he was in very close touch with everything that went on at the Park. I think his business was always secondary to football in his life. Football, and Celtic, were first and foremost with him. Even on a Saturday he would be there hours before the game, and on a Sunday he would be in at the Park again. We would all sit down in the dressing room and have a post mortem on the previous day's game or talk about what had happened elsewhere in Scotland. And in England too. Not every manager would do that with his chairman, but there was a bond between those two, and the chairman didn't interfere.

Tony McGuinness The relationship with Bob Kelly was very close, so much so that they were almost like a father and son. Jock told me once that in all the years they were together at Celtic they had had remarkably few rows, and we are talking here about two strong-willed individuals!

They both liked to get their own way, however. The only times they would have cross words was maybe when Jock was trying to get money out of the board for a player that he thought would do a job for the team.

It was funny, you know, but back in those days the team was always picked on a Thursday night, and then it was put before the board meeting for discussion. The directors always met at Celtic Park every Thursday. It's the kind of thing you would never see happening now – but that was how it was, and it was how the chairman liked things.

Well, Jock didn't want that. He wanted to be his own man. Being manager meant being in charge as far as he was concerned. Before going back he told me that he had cleared that whole side of things with the chairman before agreeing to be the manager. He had to be in complete charge of all team matters. This had been agreed, and then came the first Thursday board meeting he attended.

So they talked, and the subject of the team for the next game came up and Jock just told them that so-and-so has a knock and this other player has a strain. And there's another player who has a bit of a cold, so he wouldn't be picking the team until just before the game. The chairman looked at him and then said: 'What you're really saying is that we should mind our own business . . .' And Jock said 'Yes' and he was never asked for the team again on a Thursday night at a board meeting.

Jean He got on really well with the chairman. They were both men who spoke their minds, of course, and I suppose they respected that about each other. Bob Kelly used to talk about 'fitba people' and they were the people the pair of them liked to be with. They wanted to be talking about football all the time: morning, noon and night they would have been at it. But when he said he would go back to the Park, he stipulated that *he* would pick the team. It was agreed. To be honest, if the chairman hadn't given him that assurance, then he would not have been there.

Sean Fallon It was not everyone Bob Kelly would have given up his own power for. And he did do that. It was basically because of the respect he had for Jock. You see, previously the chairman would tell Mr McGrory which players he would like to see in the team. There would be a lot of strange team selections, and Celtic were renowned for the shock sides which were sometimes put out. I had suffered from that myself in my own playing days because the chairman wanted me played as a centre forward and I hated it. The idea behind it was that I was up there to try to upset the defence, and I didn't like the position one little bit. But I had to play there for quite a little spell because that's what Bob Kelly wanted.

When Jock returned as the manager, all of that changed and I don't think Bob regretted for one moment giving up that bit of power he had over the team. He would still come into the dressing room before a game and wish the players luck. And maybe, if it was raining and the pitch was greasy, he would say something like 'Good conditions for shooting, today, Jock'. And that was it – they'd have that kind of a little joke, but he never once interfered in any of the team selections as far as I knew. Jock wouldn't have allowed it – but, equally, the chairman didn't want a say in any of that any longer.

George Stein When it came to his job he was egotistical. He did believe that he was the best at that job. That's a natural thing, I would think, especially in the highly competitive role he was in for so long. But none of that was allowed to intrude into the family life.

When he took over at Celtic as manager it was a hard time for us, and maybe the privacy he liked became a little bit of a passion with us all: it seemed to rub off on us. I know that I shied away from being his son, or rather, from letting people know that I was Jock Stein's son. I never meant that in any bad or disrespectful way. I just wanted to be my own person, in my own right, if you like. I think he approved of that attitude.

His own happiest times were, without any doubt, his early managerial years with Celtic. I think that he probably achieved everything he ever wanted to achieve in that spell with the club. It just seemed then that everything he did was the right thing. Nothing could go wrong for him.

Jimmy Reid Those early times when Jock was the manager with Celtic were important and significant times for the whole of Scottish football. Celtic had always been a non-denominational club when it came to signing players. But with Stein there it became more than that. In the Stein years you would find people at Celtic games who had never been attracted to the club before. But they would be there on the European and other big nights. During his time as manager they were well on their way to having a non-denominational following, and a very large one at that. They were attracting fans from all over the country for games like the European Cup semi-final at Hampden against Leeds United when it seemed that every football fan in Scotland wanted to be there.

It wasn't just that Stein's teams won trophies and titles – they won them with style. Real style. There was a buccaneering spirit about them because they attacked all of the time. Stein knew what people wanted to see.

Sean Fallon He was always an optimist. There was never a time that he allowed himself to get too pessimistic about anything. If there was one thing he conveyed to the players above anything it was confidence . . . because he knew that the key to the game and to the players' performances was confidence!

He used to tell the players that they were better than anyone else. He used to drill that into them until they were believing it themselves. It was something he developed early in his career and he kept it all the way through to the end. But besides these little psychological touches there was a lot of hard work put into the job. I've never known anyone who would work harder than Jock. He would be at the Park seven days a week . . . and he expected that from everyone on the staff.

John Clark Apart from the tactical knowledge – and that was unrivalled – he had an amazingly strong personality. He would make you believe that you were as good as anyone else in the game. He would never build up the opposition too much, but he would tell you how good you were!

That helped your confidence, and his sheer presence helped you as well. He had this special kind of presence that, no matter where he was, if he walked into a room then people would turn their heads, would look at him and would realise that he was someone important. I've seen that happen in all kinds of surroundings, not just on football occasions. People who didn't know he was Jock Stein, manager of Celtic or Scotland or whatever, would recognise that this man was special. All of that rubbed off on us when he came to Celtic and, in fact, I think it rubbed off on all of his teams.

Mainly, of course, he was tactically far ahead of anyone else in the game in Scotland at that time. He added a new dimension to the game when he was a young manager. He made us talk and think about the game much more than we had ever done before. He had done that when we were youngsters, and when he came back it was as if he just started from where he had left off all those years before. What he achieved was incredible. No one else could have done it, and no one else will ever repeat it. He was streets ahead of any of the other managers in Scotland, and probably in England too. He changed everything.

Jean He lived for football. Even when we were on holiday it was as if he were counting the days until he could get back amongst it all again. I'm telling you, he thought more of the players than he thought of the rest of us. He was always trying to help them and look after them – even away from the Park he would try to make sure they were all right.

George He would travel the length and breadth of the country to see games or just to see and speak to people in the game. He would go to places like Stirling when Bob Shankly was there just so he would be able to sit and talk about football.

He loved being around 'fitba people' as he called them. I suppose my mum sometimes felt a bit constrained about all of that. The house we lived in then wasn't the safest, and she used to worry about it being left empty because he was out just about every night of the week at games. I was in my early teens and I just saw it as part of his job. Maybe there were times when we didn't think he needed to go to watch some meaningless reserve match, but they were never meaningless to him. When he was there he would probably pick up some little bit of information which would be valuable to him. He knew what was going on everywhere in the game, and I imagine that gave him better insights about what he was doing himself at Celtic.

I suppose, on the family side, he didn't have as much time for us as he had had earlier because so much was happening for him and for the club, particularly in the early years. I was always able to accept that. Basically, football was his life. Without the game his life would have been very much poorer, and I'm not talking in financial terms here. I mean the quality of his life.

Ray Stein He wasn't always around the house the way some men would be – and yet he spoiled all of us in one way or another. I think he was trying to give us a better life than the one he had known himself when he was young. He wanted all of us to be comfortable. He would bring us presents, and when he was at home he liked nothing more than having the family round about. We were always very close as a family, and that was because of my dad, I think. He didn't make close friends easily and so the family was important to him.

Jimmy Flax He was better than MI5 when it came to knowing what was going on in the game. He knew every little thing about every club and all the players in the country. Nothing went by him at all. People would phone him to tell him things – it was like an intelligence network he had going for him. He was ahead of them all. He knew everything. If there was something he didn't know, then it wasn't worth knowing.

Tony McGuinness You know, he would take on a whole lot that went far beyond his job as team manager. He helped out so many players who had off-field problems. He helped them through domestic and financial problems – anything that was worrying them. I suppose he reckoned that a problem-free player would be better for the team.

A whole lot of them would never have lasted as long in the game as they did if it had not been for the help and the advice that he gave them. There are ex-players who are still grateful for all the things he did for them – and not just in a football sense. He was never done helping players. They owed him so much.

Jimmy Johnstone I don't think any other manager in football could have done as much for me as Big Jock did. Everything Celtic has become is down to him: he made the club what it is today. There's no doubt about that. Sure, there were good players when he arrived to take over as manager, but we were not winning things. He changed that, and when we won the European Cup Celtic became a big, big name in world football. Before that we had been known in Scotland and down south, but no one bothered too much about Celtic on the Continent. He brought that extra fame, and it still exists today because of him.

Tony Queen No one will ever be able to repeat what he did in his years with Celtic. His record will stand forever. That's his monument. Nine titles in succession, and then all the Cups, the League Cups, and above all the European Cup. Apart from the record, the team he built was something else. We'll never see the likes of the Lisbon Lions again. There was just something about that team. People can talk as much as they like about great club sides, but I don't think you'll ever get one better than that Lisbon team. You have to remember that the Italians were dominating the European scene then with that defensive football which was killing the game. Then the Big Man came along and showed how the game should be played. Celtic were a breath of fresh air back in those days. They showed that exciting, attacking football could still be successful. The fact that they won that European Cup was a great thing for the whole game. I'm not saying that because he was a pal of mine – the facts speak for themselves. He is down in history, and there's no one deserves to be there more than the Big Man.

Margaret McDade My mother used to worry about all the games he was involved in. But she wouldn't listen to them on the radio or watch them on the telly when they were actually taking place. She would only look at them after she knew John had won.

On the day of the European Cup Final in Lisbon she got herself in a real state. She was up to high doh and eventually she went off to her bed at two o'clock in the afternoon, well ahead of the kick-off time. She took sleeping pills so that she would get to sleep and then she slept her way right through the match. When she wakened and we told her that Celtic had beaten Inter Milan and that they had won the European Cup she just told us all that she had always known that 'her John' was going to win that Cup. She was so proud of him and so sure of him.

Sean Fallon People sometimes talk about Lisbon as if it simply happened overnight. But nothing as important as that can happen without a whole lot of hard work going into it. Our work had started back the previous summer when Jock had decided to take the team to the States and Canada after winning the championship. He began to plan it all then, and I can remember him telling me that we would need a bigger pool of players if we were going to do anything in the European Cup. I think maybe we had thirteen or fourteen players who were really good enough, and he wanted to have sixteen or seventeen. On that trip we ran short of players, and Neilly Mochan and myself almost had to make comebacks in the last match against a Mexican team in Los Angeles. That brought it home to Jock that he had to get more players and that's when he started to plan for the European Cup. He was always thinking ahead, always looking to the future and trying to make sure that the team would be ready for whatever challenge they had to face. He was able to foresee things, solving problems for the team way before they were happening. He never stopped thinking about the game. That's why he was always that bit ahead of any of his rivals.

John Clark Of all the memories we had as players, Lisbon was the greatest. It will always be that way for the lads who played in the game against Inter. There was an innocence about all of us then. I don't think that any of us could quite believe that we were in the European Cup Final. This was a game we watched on TV – we never imagined for a minute that we would be playing in it. We stayed in Estoril at the Palacio Hotel and there seemed to be celebrities about the place the whole time. But Big Jock was scarcely ever away from us. He was with the players the whole time during the build-up to that game. In the afternoons we would have card schools, just a couple of pounds or so changing hands, and he would take part in them. It was as if he didn't want to leave us on our own. He was trying to make sure that we were not going to be under pressure. And he succeeded in protecting us from the pressures which can affect teams preparing for big games.

I can remember di Stefano, the greatest player of his time and a man who had dominated the competition we were trying to win, coming to the hotel. He arrived to ask Celtic to play in his testimonial match against Real Madrid in the Bernebeu Stadium. Big Jock saw him, spoke to him and then was back among us as soon as the arrangements for the game had been made.

It was just that he was watching out for us. We had to stay in the shade as much as possible because it was warm and he was worried in case anyone would get too much sun. In a way, he fathered us.

Ray Lisbon was a high spot for my dad, but I don't remember that day as much as I remember the night he won the Scottish Cup with Dunfermline. There was so much hassle about Lisbon, travelling there on the morning of the game and all that. But without any doubt that was his day. Yet I can remember when our plane home was postponed and I had to call him from the airport in the middle of the night. I woke him up. You know, he had had to take sleeping pills to get to sleep because of all the excitement of the day. And when I spoke to him so that arrangements could be made for all of us – I was on the flight with the players' wives – he didn't even know he had won the European Cup. I think it had all been too much for him.

Jimmy Johnstone The one thing about Lisbon was how he had us all believing that we were every bit as good as Inter Milan. There was no way that he was going to allow us on the field that day with any kind of inferiority complex. We went out of the dressing room that day singing the Celtic song. I don't think the Italians knew what was happening. They thought we were all crazy, but he had us relaxed and ready for that game.

Sean Fallon Jock was always a great psychologist. He wanted to show the players that they didn't have to worry about Inter and all the glamour which surrounded them. And so, when the two teams were meant to go out together, Jock just sent our lads out first because we had the biggest number of supporters there and he wanted our lads to see and recognise that – and he wanted the Italians to know it as well.

We went out right after the team, Jock walked straight to the nearest bench, and that was when the fun began – because Helenio Herrera, Inter Milan's coach, wanted that seat. But Jock was determined that he wasn't going to budge for anyone, especially Herrera.

Now, Jock knew that the players and the fans would be watching this, and it was really a battle of wills. Herrera ordered us to get up, and Jock just gave him one of those looks and told him to 'get the hell out of it' in his best Lanarkshire accent. I don't think Herrera needed an interpreter for that message. You should have seen Herrera's face! He was a very arrogant man, and he thought he was the king pin. Maybe too many people went along with that, but Big Jock didn't, and it was important for us to assert ourselves in that way. It let everyone know that we were not going to be pushed around. It was a clever psychological blow, but Jock was always good at that side of things.

Lawrie McMenemy He was the Scot who was the first manager in Britain to win the European Cup that day in Lisbon, and no one deserved that honour more than he did. Jock was an ordinary man who was extraordinary when it came to football. There are a lot of 'big men' in football, but there was only one Big Man – that was Jock.

The phrase might have been coined for him and him alone. No one in world football was more successful than Jock Stein. No one.

What he achieved at Celtic could never have been achieved by anyone else; only Jock with that miner's toughness and that street-wise knowledge he used so many times to such advantage for his teams. He was so good, so far ahead of any other manager, that I sometimes think that we all took his successes too much for granted. That day in Lisbon was a major victory – but it was only part of his astonishing career.

Tony Queen In all that European Cup run he played only one game defensively, and that was in Prague when they played the Army team Dukla. Stevie Chalmers must have run a hundred miles that night because he was the only forward up the field. It went against Jock's beliefs to do that, but it was a semi-final and he desperately wanted to win that European Cup. He got the result he wanted in Czechoslovakia – but he would have preferred to play the game in another way. He told me that often enough. But it was the one time he used those tactics in all the games they played that season. They won everything, remember, every single competition they took part in. Not just that European Cup – every trophy there was, the lot. That showed the stature of the man.

Of course there was never any way that he would lower his sights. He was not the kind of man to settle for second place if he thought that the team could take first place in everything. Actually Lisbon was a crazy day for me. There I was over there supporting Celtic and going daft about them winning the Cup, and it was costing me ten grand back home. There was a wee punter who worked out in the Hoover factory in Cambuslang, Welsh was his name I think, and he had bet on Celtic winning everything. I had laid him odds of 200–1, and it came up for him. I was never as happy paying out on a big bet as I was that time. It was a great, great day for the club and for the supporters and for Big Jock. But it didn't stop there with him, did it? He just went on and on winning titles and cups year after year.

Jimmy Flax If you look back at those years he had with the Celtic you get a flavour of what he did. But being there at the time it was just too much at times. We had had all of these bad years and now suddenly we were the best team in Europe. That's what Jock did for Celtic and for all of us who followed the team.

Lisbon was the greatest game of all. That even put the 7–1 win over Rangers in the shade. They went out there and played as if it was just another game. It was unbelievable the way they set about that Italian mob. You have to remember, too, that Inter Milan were supposed to be unbeatable. The thing is, nobody told Big Jock that.

Guys gave up their jobs and everything just to get there. As well as the players I think he was able to convince all of us that we were going to win that Cup that year. I remember flying over with my old pal Donny Sutherland. We used to go everywhere together, and that particular time was the best. I think the Big Man thought so too.

John Clark It's right that we should all remember Lisbon, but we were close to winning a European trophy a year earlier – after Big Jock had been manager for just a year. We had won the Scottish Cup and automatically qualified for the European Cup Winners' Cup as a result of that win over Dunfermline at Hampden. He worked on us, added one or two fresh faces, and we reached the semi-final of that tournament. We beat a Dutch team, Go Ahead of Deventer, in the first round and then Aarhus of Denmark before knocking out Dynamo Kiev in the quarter-finals. Then we took on Liverpool and they beat us by just one goal in the semi-final. We were unlucky because a Bobby Lennox goal was disallowed at Anfield in that tie. The final was at Hampden that year, and Borussia Dortmund would never have beaten us in Glasgow.

Sean Fallon They were all great achievements in those

years. But the European Cup win was the ultimate because it proved that boys born and bred in Scotland could go out there and beat the cream of Europe. That Inter Milan team cost millions to put together and they came from all over the place – all our players were Scottish, and it was a long, long time before any team could boast of winning that trophy with players of just the one nationality.

But there were the nine championships in a row as well, and that will never be equalled. To win the title you have to show consistency over the whole season – to do that for nine years, well you look back and wonder sometimes how it was possible. I don't think Jock ever visualised that. No one could. The old chairman used to go on about the time when Celtic won seven in a row between 1904 and 1911; he could remember that and he used to preach to us about it. But I don't believe the chairman really thought it could happen again.

Lawrie McMenemy I remember sitting with Jock at a testimonial dinner for Bobby Murdoch in Middlesbrough. Jock was very much the focal point of the evening, which was usually the case with him because of that fantastic presence he always had. Anyhow, he had given a medal to the organisers to auction for Bobby. It was a Scottish Championship medal and the bidding rose and rose. It went beyond modest and really well beyond any expectations the organisers had had for it. I can't remember exactly what it was sold for, but it was around £1000. As the value increased by the minute Jock leaned over to me and said, 'Bloody hell, I've got ten more of these at home!'

Ten more! It was remarkable. No manager should ever be able to control the destiny of a single club so completely as that – yet Jock did. That was a measure of the man's greatness. I am not interested in whether he did it in Scotland, England or Northern Ireland, that doesn't matter. To be able to produce that kind of dominance for your club for so long is not just exceptional but near miraculous. And it was ninety per cent down to his vitality,

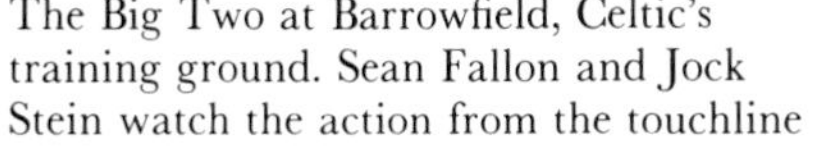

The Big Two at Barrowfield, Celtic's training ground. Sean Fallon and Jock Stein watch the action from the touchline

Jock Stein with daughter Ray on her wedding day

A proud mother and father meet son George at the airport after he had been on tour with Celtic's Boys Club

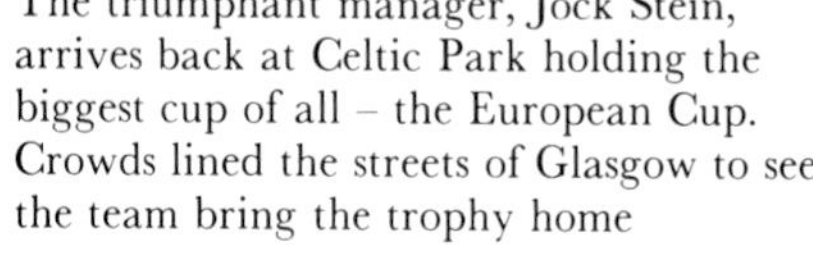

The triumphant manager, Jock Stein, arrives back at Celtic Park holding the biggest cup of all – the European Cup. Crowds lined the streets of Glasgow to see the team bring the trophy home

Jimmy Johnstone – Celtic and Scotland. Jock Stein used to keep an eye on his off-field activities

Tommy Gemmell equalizes against Inter Milan in the 1967 European Cup final. Celtic, of course, went on to their famous victory

Some of the Lisbon Lions 11 years on, reunited at Jock Stein's testimonial match. *Left to right*: Willie Wallace, Billy McNeill, Bobby Murdoch, Steve Chalmers, John Hughes (partially hidden), Jock Stein, Tommy Gemmell, John Clark and Jim Craig

Jock Stein presents his former Celtic captain Kenny Dalglish with the trophy after Liverpool's victory over Celtic in Stein's testimonial game at Parkhead

Badly behaved fans got short shrift from Stein

Stein congratulates the players after yet another Hampden win

his grasp of management and his complete enthusiasm for the game. He was just the best at his job. The very best.

George When he went to Lisbon for the European Cup Final he didn't seem afraid of the game with Inter at all. It didn't appear to be worrying him one little bit. It was funny – this was the game of his, and of the players', lives and yet he wasn't worried by it. He could be like that at times, have hunches, and somehow deep down be sure that he was going to win. I had difficulty understanding that side of him because I was always more negative in my outlook on things. I could always see clouds on the horizon.

He just seemed able to blow all of those clouds away. I think I worried about him more than he worried about himself; and that goes for everyone in the family. The win in Lisbon meant a great deal to him personally as well as for the club.

It was funny the way his hunches worked. I can remember one league game against Rangers at Ibrox. At this time I had been more or less banned from going there because of the possibility of trouble. Not actually banned – but certainly not allowed to go to the Old Firm games there. Then one time he came into the house on the Friday night and asked me, very casually, 'Are you going to the game tomorrow?' I told him that he would not allow me to go and hadn't allowed me for a little while and then he just said, 'Go tomorrow because we are going to win.' Now this was an early season game and Celtic were not expected to win, but he thought they would; he had this feeling, this hunch, that they would, and he wanted me to be there to see it. I went, his hunch was right, and Celtic won 1–0. I think it was their first win in the league at Ibrox for a dozen years but he was so sure that they would do it. When he was like that you were better not trying to argue with him.

Jean It was always hard to enjoy the games when John was involved as the manager. I used to sit in the stand and worry about how the games would go. I suppose

Lisbon was one of the best memories he had – but there were so many memories from these days with Celtic. For John there was always something special about winning. He was a very bad loser. I've seen him come in on a Saturday night and be in his bed at twenty minutes past six. That was me left to watch the television all night because he wasn't going anywhere because he had lost the match.

Jessie McNeill Jean used to say that he would go into hiding when he was beaten. Well, he didn't hide that often because he didn't get beat all that often. Particularly in the early years with Celtic.

Jimmy Reid It has to be acknowledged that Jock Stein was undoubtedly, undoubtedly the one product of Scottish football during my lifetime who was accepted as one of the all-time greats internationally. Nine titles in succession, ten out of eleven – I didn't think that was possible. It is a measure of the stranglehold he imposed on Scottish football as a whole. I don't think it was necessarily good for the game generally – certainly not after the fifth or sixth time. But Celtic supporters would deny that vehemently, I know that.

But when you sit back and look at the broader picture, at the game in Scotland as a whole, it was not a good thing. It became a monopoly of the First Division Championship and one made possible by Jock Stein. He worked this kind of miracle with basically the same players who had been there before he arrived and had not been able to win anything. What he brought to Celtic will never be repeated there, or anywhere else. He made them a world name.

Sean Fallon That season we won the European Cup in Lisbon, well we had a clean sweep of everything, and I think maybe sometimes people push that into the background because the European Cup was so big and we were the first British team to win it. But there was a lot of hard work put in that season, and the pressure just mounted week after week after week until it was finally all over that day in Portugal.

Jimmy Flax One of his secrets was that he knew what every man could do and what he couldn't do. And so, even in the European Cup Final itself, he never asked a single one of his players to do a job he wasn't capable of doing.

John Clark Later in his life, much later, I used to go to games with him, and one time we had gone up to Aberdeen to watch a match there. In fact it might have been the last time I saw him alive. We went to see Aberdeen against Dundee United, and on the way back he was talking about the good days with Celtic and reminiscing about all the players who had been there around the Lisbon era. I'll always remember he said: 'The great thing about all of you in that team was that you could train – really train hard. I used to try to gut you at times on the training ground but not one of you would give in.' He was hard and he was demanding but he always wanted the best for us all.

His was the major contribution and no one can ever deny that, but he would be the first to say the backroom staff helped him. There were Sean and Neilly Mochan, Alex Boden, John Higgins, Willie Fernie – a lot of them. But he was the man. The era of the Lisbon Lions was *the* time for him. He used to talk about these days often and he said that Bobby Murdoch was the best player he ever handled. He told me that several times and then he would add, 'But you were all good . . .'

Sometimes people talk of the Lisbon Lions and think only of the eleven players who played that day. That's wrong, and I'm saying this as one of the eleven. Other players made big, big contributions to the successes we had that season.

One was Joe McBride, who was the best finisher I ever saw, but whose career was curtailed halfway through that season because of injury. Then there was John Hughes, a personality player if ever there was one, and Charlie

Gallacher, Willie O'Neill, John Cushley, all of them did a bit. But while all of us did a bit here and there it was Big Jock's contribution which brought the club success. Not success which only lasted a short time, but the kind which established Celtic as a major name in the game right across the world. Before him they were known in Scotland, England and Ireland, and also in the States and Canada because of the exiled fans there, but it was only after Jock Stein arrived that the club became known world-wide in the real sense. What Celtic are today is a direct result of what Jock Stein did for the club. No one should ever argue with that.

OK, maybe when he arrived at the Park it was the stage he needed himself at that time in his career. He had been at Dunfermline and Hibs, both smaller clubs, and this was a chance for him. But he would have been a success without Celtic. Celtic, however, would not have been a success without him.

George There seems to have grown up a kind of unwillingness among some people to recognise my dad's achievements. It exists among some of the people at Celtic Park today and it upsets me a lot. In some of the documentaries which were done about the European Cup win it was as if his role was being downgraded a little bit. Not obviously, but in a subtle way, like people saying how lucky he was to go to Celtic when all those good players were there. My dad would never have argued with the fact that there were good players at Parkhead when he took over. He knew that, and was the first to say it, and I accept that too. But they hadn't exactly known any success before he returned. Celtic brought him back from the job he had at Easter Road because they needed someone who would give them that success. He gave it to them – more than they ever dreamed of.

There were other good managers around at that time, and maybe one of them could have brought more out of the players too – but I doubt if any of them could have done what he did.

You would also have to look at the other clubs he had managed. Had there been good players at Dunfermline just waiting for him, and good players at Hibs just sitting around until he was made manager? He won the Scottish Cup at Dunfermline and he won the Summer Cup with Hibs and then took them to the Scottish Cup semi-final in the year he left to go back to Celtic. Also, how did all the good players get on when they left Celtic, when they were transferred? Did any of them have the same kind of success they had under my dad? I don't think so.

Tony McGuinness I can only presume that, at times, it was jealousy talking when you heard people try to belittle what the Big Man had done for Celtic. Often it was people who should have known better who tried to do it: people from inside the club, who were jealous of what he had done, and jealous of the fact that the supporters realised it was Jock who had done it. It was the support which always counted with him in any case, and they recognised him as the founder, if you like, of the club as it was when the European Cup was won, when the nine titles in succession were won, and of everything that has come since in terms of the club's standing in world football.

Jimmy Reid I personally think that the unique contributions and achievements of Jock Stein in terms of football are not yet fully appreciated in Scotland. I think it's not just the bare statistics that are all-important – it is the quality of all that he did. There was genuine quality in the way all his teams played. There were so many things to be admired.

When Celtic beat Inter Milan in Lisbon, it became a kind of renaissance for the game as it should be played. The Italians had concentrated almost totally on defence. Their *cattanaccio* system was suffocating the game and stifling the skills of players. Jock saw that as being something he did not believe in and did not approve of. He attacked that day because that was what he wanted to do, to restore attacking football in all its glory. He succeeded.

People throughout Europe celebrated the defeat of *cattanaccio*. A friend of mine in Budapest sent me a letter shortly after that game in Lisbon to tell me that youngsters playing in the parks there were all wanting to be Jimmy Johnstone. There they were identifying with Scottish players, with Celtic players, and in Hungary Jock Stein's name was being invoked because of his triumph in Lisbon. There he was being praised in the nation which had inspired him so much in the fifties as he developed his own football philosophy.

Yet here, in this small country of Scotland, people have tried to chip away at his outstanding achievements. He has not been given full credit for all of them, and for all of what he did for his country. Eventually he will get that recognition. He will have to. I am sure of that.

Jimmy Flax Sometimes I wonder what it would have been like if the Big Man had never gone back to Celtic. I shudder when I think of that because I can remember the days before he was there. Maybe too many people have forgotten them, but the supporters haven't – they know what he did for the club.

John Clark He had this ability to convince you that you were as good as, or better than, anyone else in the game. No one could teach him a thing about football management. He had it all. That's why people phoned him from everywhere asking for advice or information. And when it came to information he had an intelligence service which could not be bettered.

Anyone who played under him had some kind of success. At Dunfermline, at Hibs, and especially at Celtic – they all had something which he gave to them. He put clubs and players on the map. They were in the limelight because of what he did for them.

Jean He had more confidence about himself when he went to Celtic because he had had the earlier times with

Dunfermline and Hibs. I believe that he *knew*, really knew, that he would get Celtic success again. He didn't have to say that in the house. I can remember him saying that he was meeting Bob Kelly and he had the chance to go back there, and the way he said it I knew that was what he wanted. And I knew, too, that he would make a go of it. Maybe he didn't think he would win all he did win, but he knew that he would make Celtic a top team again. There was always that kind of conviction about John.

Ray The time was right for him to go to Celtic and the set-up was right for him, too. He had a strong relationship with the chairman and had known Sean Fallon since they had been players together.

He loved being there, just being back at the Park. And then he had all the success. Sean was exactly the right man to be my dad's assistant in those good days. He provided the perfect balance and my dad knew he could rely on him. You need the right mix in management team and the partnership definitely worked.

Jimmy Reid His truly international reputation always impressed me, as did his way with players.

He had such clarity of thought. Any tactics he developed were always with his players in mind. By that I mean that he would not try to fit players into some framework which did not suit them. He would look at his players and devise tactics which would fully utilise their skills. Duke Ellington used to set a framework around the soloists of his orchestra – rather than forcing them to fit the arrangements, and Jock did much the same in football. Maybe Jock was the Duke Ellington of football. Or Duke was the Jock Stein of jazz!

To go back to the international aspect of his reputation, I can remember once being asked to accept an award on his behalf from the English Football Writers because for some reason Jock could not go to London himself. While there I met Helmut Schoen, the great West German international team boss, and he explained why I was at the

6
Some setbacks . . .

For almost the whole of that charmed career with Celtic, charmed both for Stein and for the club whose rebirth he made possible, it was non-stop success.

Only twice during his incredible reign at Parkhead did Celtic fail to have a trophy gleaming in the board room. And on one of these occasions Stein had been the victim of a car crash which kept him out of football for a whole season.

For the rest of the time Jock Stein gathered titles the way other football managers gathered sackings. He collected cups and medals at a rate no one had ever come close to equalling – and yet there were setbacks and there were disappointments. Even that idyllic career was scarred by some failures.

They were failures to Stein – they might have been successes to other managers.

Failure to win a World Club Championship against Racing Club of Argentina was one . . .

Failure to win a *second* European Cup when the team lost to Feyenoord was another . . .

To reach a final might have been enough for some men. For Stein, who wanted to win everything he was involved in, they were failures.

And there were other setbacks, too, before the last, sad days of his career as the most successful club manager the game has ever known.

Sean Fallon The World Championship game in South

America was the one time that Bob Kelly and Jock had a serious difference of opinion on the way that the club should go about things. It was always very important to Bob the manner in which you won a game. He was strong on discipline and so was Jock. And then things went wrong over there in Montevideo.

We had beaten Racing Club of Argentina at Hampden in the first game 1–0. Now this was a two-legged match we had been asked to take part in by UEFA because we were European club champions and they wanted an annual match with the South American club champions. But we travelled to the return game worried after the way the Argentinian players had behaved at Hampden. Poor Ronnie Simpson was knocked out by a bottle at the warm-up for the match in Buenos Aires, and although we scored first we eventually lost 2–1 – and that's when a third game was ordered.

It was also when the trouble came between Jock and the chairman. Bob wanted to go home straightaway. He didn't want to have to play the third game with all the potential for trouble there was. Initially the chairman simply said, that's it, we are not going to Uruguay to play the third match. But Jock wanted to play. He always wanted to win, and we knew that, but also he didn't want it to look as if Celtic would not fulfil their obligations as the European representatives. He didn't want to be accused of running away.

So Jock spoke to the other directors and he worked on the chairman too and eventually he got his way. But it wasn't the right way, as the later happenings proved.

John Clark South America hurt him. I think it hurt him more deeply than he ever let on. It came just a few months after we had been winning praise for the European Cup victory in Lisbon – and then suddenly we were being pilloried. He didn't like that one bit.

The image of the club was tarnished by all of what went on out there on the field in that third game, and he hated that to happen at any time. He wanted the club to look good at all times. That was primary in his thinking. But we had had a hostile crowd to face, a hostile press and hostile players. Remember this was not so very long after the Argentinians had been described by Sir Alf Ramsey as 'animals'. That was in the World Cup quarter-final at Wembley just eighteen months earlier, when Rattin had been sent off against England. OK, we were Scottish, but in Buenos Aires they identified us with England and with Sir Alf, and so they wanted to take revenge on us – and they didn't mess about. The same thing was to happen to other teams after us who played in that fixture, but we were the first to be involved in trouble and we came out of the whole thing badly. Looking back down the years it's very easy to say that we were wrong, but it was not as easy or as simple as that. There were just so many problems surrounding that fixture, on and off the field. Maybe we should not have gone to play the third game but we wanted to play. We wanted to be world champions.

Jimmy Johnstone I was sent off in the game for retaliating. But there is a limit to what you can take on the park, and the referee from Paraguay was not protecting us. My hair was soaked in spittle because their players just kept spitting on me all the time. If they kicked you they would come over and make out that they were apologising. They would pat your head as if to say sorry, but they were really pulling your hair. They were just totally callous and cynical.

Ray Stein I was there in South America, and I don't think I've ever seen a more hostile crowd. I really worried for the safety of the players. When Ronnie Simpson was hit by a bottle from the crowd I think everyone knew what Celtic were in for. In the end they took the brunt of the bad publicity, but what happened in the third game when the Celtic players were ordered off was not the whole story. I know that my dad wanted to play the third game – he wouldn't walk away from a crowd of hooligans, his nature would never have allowed him to do that, but I know he regretted it. It was so hard to have to accept that criticism so soon after winning the European Cup.

Sean Fallon Jock admitted after the third game that he had been wrong to insist on playing in Montevideo. By then, after all the dust had settled, I think all of us recognised that the chairman had been right. That hurt them both, you know. Big Jock didn't like it when the club received bad publicity and everyone seemed to be after us because of the players being ordered off and all. And the chairman, well, he had gone from the happiest day of his life, standing in the Palacio Hotel with the European Cup by his side, to this inside six months. He was really disappointed and saddened by the whole thing.

George Stein The worst thing about that whole business of the World Club Championship was the trouble it brought on the club. Dad didn't like the club's name to be dragged through the dirt. That's why there were those times when he went on to the terracings himself to break up trouble. He did it at Arbroath and at Stirling Albion, just going in among the trouble-makers and sorting them out. So when it was trouble on the field which brought the club bad publicity, then clearly it was upsetting to him. In fact, he hated it.

Sean Fallon Discipline had always been important to him, and if there were any breaches of discipline then they were dealt with quietly. It was something else he had learned from Bob. The chairman used to talk about keeping everything in the family. A lot of things happened but no one would find out about them unless he wanted them to.

This time, after the South American business, then the club did go public and the chairman held a press conference and announced that the players were all being fined £250 each. I think the chairman and Jock agreed that, because of all the publicity, this time people had to know the punishments being given to the players. It was a sad time at the club.

John Clark That was one of the rare occasions when

anyone was fined by the Big Man. And, really, it was the club who were doing it. I mean he hated anyone being late, and he hated any kind of indiscipline, but he wouldn't fine players all that often. He took the view that the lads were all family men with young children, and to take money off them, to take money out of their wages, would be hurting their families. He had other ways to hit players who had displeased him in one way or another. On the training ground was one of his favourite spots – he would get you out there and hammer you if you had done something wrong.

Being late was one of the worst sins for him. He used to crack up at players who were late. I can remember once wee Bertie Auld missed the train when we were going to an away game in Edinburgh. He didn't wait for the next train – he took a taxi through so that he would be there at the same time as the rest of the team. Well, Big Jock had him out in front of the players and praised him for his initiative. He told him how well he had done to jump in a taxi and get through to Edinburgh as quickly as he had done. Then he added, 'But it's not going to do you any good – you're sitting in the stand.' He would not put up with a whole team standing around waiting for one individual who was late. It didn't matter who it was either.

The South American trouble was a blot on our good name for a time – but it wasn't lasting. There were still good days in front of him. And for the club too of course.

George The season might have ended in a bit of an anti-climax in 1970 when Celtic lost to Feyenoord in the final of the European Cup that season. But earlier it contained two results which were special landmarks for my dad. According to everyone in England, Leeds United were en route to winning the European Cup that season when they were drawn against Celtic in the semi-finals. They had the best team they had ever had, they had won the title the previous year to go into Europe's top tournament, and they had vast European experience from the other competitions.

But so did Celtic, and so did my dad. He enjoyed all of that, especially the battle of wits with his mate Don Revie. Leeds were a very thorough team, but when they were watching Celtic before the semi-finals my dad was shifting players around so they didn't know what was going to hit them. Apparently they couldn't work out how Celtic were going to approach the games. Of course, my dad loved that kind of thing. He enjoyed keeping the opposition guessing, and he had a strong pool of players he could use to continue to get results in Scotland and clinch the championship before the first match with Leeds.

Anyhow, Leeds were built up to be invincible, and that was the type of challenge my dad loved. Celtic went to Elland Road and won 1–0 with a goal from George Connelly. That was when the excuses began to pour in. Poor Leeds had too many games to play, they had a pile of injuries to worry them. Celtic had a similar fixture list, and they also had the odd injury or two. But in any case, I remember Leeds were able to field all of their big names when the second leg was played at Hampden. There were 136,505 people in the ground that night and they saw Leeds score first and then saw Celtic score two goals and win the second game as well. The result was played down in England, but Celtic had beaten them over *two* games, winning each one and generally outplaying them. It was one of his greatest triumphs and he loved every moment.

Tony Queen Normally in his team talks before big games he would point out this or that to the likes of Billy McNeill or Bobby Murdoch or Bertie Auld, and wee Jinky [Jimmy Johnstone] would just be sitting there with the rest, whistling away and not listening to a word. At the end of the talk the wee Barra would say, 'Hey, Boss, you never told me anything.' And the Big Man would just tell him, 'You go out there and do whatever the hell you like.' That was the way he spoke to Jinky. You couldn't really tell him what to do because he had so much talent . . . he destroyed Leeds didn't he?

Jimmy Johnstone Before the first game against Leeds at Elland Road we were staying in a hotel out in Harrogate, and that's where we had the team talk. And how he embarrassed me in front of the rest of the lads that day. Usually after he had finished with the talk he would come round and have a quiet word with me or with someone else and gee us up that way. This time he told the rest of the lads in the team that I would be the match winner. He went on and on about how I would do this and that to Terry Cooper, who was England's left back at the time. I could feel my face going red and I couldn't look at the rest of the lads when he finished. But we went out and we won and I had not a bad game.

Tony McGuinness He could lift players for certain games. He would do that with Jimmy Johnstone, for instance. There was the time when he promised wee Jimmy that he would not have to go to Belgrade if the home leg of the European Cup tie with Red Star produced enough goals to make Celtic safe. This was because the wee man hated flying. Well, Jimmy ran riot and Celtic won 5–1 – and he scored twice himself.

He did the same with the wee man before the Leeds match, and Terry Cooper was destroyed. Mind you, *no one* could handle Jinky when he was on song.

Sean Fallon Jock had a love–hate relationship with wee Jimmy. We used to look on him as a kind of a little boy lost. Off the record I'd have a word with wee Jimmy, or the Big Man would speak to him quietly, but all his brains were in his feet. The wee bugger would come in for training and you would know he had been misbehaving yet he would train as if he had been in bed at nine o'clock the night before. Then, when you were getting on at him he would look at you with those big eyes of his and you would feel sorry for him.

But whatever problems he provided were usually forgiven because he had such marvellous natural ability. He would win games for you – dozens of games he won for us in those days – and the people would go to games just to see him play. There was a special feeling between Jimmy and the fans. He was with the club from the time he was a kid, and if he had had just a little bit more self discipline there's no saying how good he would have been. He was one of the greats anyhow, but he had such ability.

Leeds was just one of his great games. They were so confident about that first-leg game down there at Elland Road. Not that Don Revie and his people were shouting about what they would do – the English newspapers were doing that – but still, Don and the rest of them were quietly confident that they would get a result to bring with them to Hampden. We surprised them, and no one had more surprises for them that night than wee Jimmy. They had a great side and they were in the running for everything that season. They were two memorable nights, two great games, but we killed each other for the final. I honestly believe that we beat each other that night for the ultimate glory. We failed against Feyenoord in the final, and if Leeds had gone through they would have done the same, because I think both teams gave everything in the two semi-final matches. That was the mistake which maybe both of us made.

Ray The final against Feyenoord seemed to be an anti-climax for everyone. Leeds had been such a contrast – the Celtic supporters just seemed to take over the town for that first leg, and then there was that huge crowd at Hampden for the second match. Maybe we all thought we had won the Cup when Leeds were beaten.

Sean Fallon Too many things went wrong for that final in Milan. The players set up a pool for off-field perks and were having meetings with an agent before the game. He was wanting various deals set up – but all this was happening before the game. I can remember the dressing room at the San Siro Stadium after we had been beaten in extra time by the Dutch team. The chairman was sitting there, and he was so disappointed. But even then, Sir Robert, as he was by that time, was more upset at the way the team had played. I can still remember him saying, 'I don't mind losing, but not the way that we lost. That was wrong for this club and its supporters. The attitude was wrong.'

But by the time Jock and I realised that, it was too late. The players were wanting to charge photographers money for pictures before we even went on to the field.

Jean Stein He felt very low after that game, and there was a tour of Canada and the States coming almost straight away when we all got back from Milan. He went, but he came home from that tour early. He didn't have his heart in it. It took him time to get over that and all the goings-on before the game.

Tony Queen I remember we organised a party for Jock and Jean when they came home after the Feyenoord game. He was leaving the next day for the States, and you could see that by this stage he really didn't want to go on that tour. But he did go, and he came to the party; he put his troubles behind him, and he was the life and soul of the place. We had hoped it was going to be a victory celebration – and it wasn't – but he still turned up and he still enjoyed himself. Of course, he was among friends that night. It was the kind of night he enjoyed where he could relax without worrying about a thing. I like to think that the party helped him, maybe it eased the hurt after all that happened in Italy. I think that was such a big disappointment because everyone had been on such a high after beating Leeds in both of the semi-final matches. That first match at Leeds when George Connelly scored in the opening minutes . . . poor George.

Jean George Connelly was a tragedy for John because he thought so much of the boy and yet he walked out on Celtic and eventually just went back to playing junior football. I can remember one night somebody phoning from Fife about some problem with George Connelly and John and Sean both went straightaway to try to sort things out. It was after one o'clock in the morning before they got home. He worried about George Connelly and he tried everything to keep him in the game and at the Park. He thought he was a great player.

George had so much ability, so much talent and then he just threw it all away. I think it was just the boy's nature, the kind of quiet person he was. He didn't want any of the hassles of football. He walked out on a Scotland team once and John nearly had a fit. He was always up at his house trying to solve whatever problems came up. Eventually, though, he just couldn't give the laddie the right answers. He was very broken up over that.

Tony McGuinness George Connelly was the one major problem Jock never solved, and that upset him. Watching so much talent going to waste made the Big Man angry. But he spent time with George Connelly because he knew that the boy had problems. George used to tell him that he wanted to be a lorry driver. He had a pal who drove a lorry and he didn't have to train every day and he didn't have to work on a Saturday, and really, when he kept up that theme there was no answer.

Jock was never away from the boy's house in Blantyre trying to save his career for him. I knew a bit about that because it was an uncle of mine who had taken George Connelly to Celtic Park in the first place. George was always a loner. His one mate at the Park was Davie Hay, and when Davie moved south to Chelsea George didn't last long after that. Yet the Big Man was convinced that he was going to be another Franz Beckenbauer. He used to say that about him, and it was a major regret for him that he couldn't persuade the boy to stay in football. He just walked out. He came back for a spell, but it was never going to be right, and eventually he disappeared from the scene altogether and went back to work in Fife.

Jean He always worried about players who were throwing their talent away. At Hibs he used to spend a lot of time with Willie Hamilton. He had his problems, but he was such a great player that John wanted to help him. He was sympathetic towards him and, for a spell, he was able to get Hamilton to show all the skills that he had. He got him into the Scotland team and he tried so hard to keep him on the straight and narrow. He would spend hours with people if he thought they were wasting the ability they had.

John Clark He never wanted any of the players to be in any trouble. He tried to be like a father to every single one of us. Some of the lads didn't like that, you know, that kind of discipline. The way he would sit in a hotel foyer making sure that no one was out late. He would sit there and he would miss nothing. Neilly Mochan used to say he could hear a fiver floating along a hotel corridor. He did all that for our own good. He wanted all of us to be right.

7

. . . and the final disappointment

In the summer of 1975 Jock Stein was almost killed in a car crash as he returned from holiday in Minorca. Also in the car were his close friends Tony Queen and Bob Shankly, Jean Stein and Shankly's wife Greta. Both Stein and Tony Queen were seriously injured in the crash.

The season before, Stein had had to content himself with third place in the League after almost a decade of non-stop success. He had, as always, better consolation prizes than anyone else would ever have looked for. Indeed, for most managers, a season which produced a League Cup win and another Scottish Cup win would have been outstandingly successful. But Stein still saw the championship as the major target, and even nine-in-a-row couldn't satisfy his hunger.

There was to be only one more championship for Stein to celebrate before his departure from Celtic.

Tony Queen The car crash took a lot out of Jock. I know how much it took out of me and I know he was the same. He came close to death after that accident, and don't forget, a couple of years or so before he had had a mild heart attack. He tried to make light of it, but it was a warning. After it he and I went up to Aviemore for a holiday. It was a break away from things and we used to walk a lot and talk a lot – but even when he was supposed to be relaxing he remained as competitive as ever. There was a snooker table in the hotel and one of these Liverpool pop groups were staying there too. Gerry and the Pacemakers, it was, and Gerry, the leader of the group, wanted to play the Big Man at snooker. Well, the guy beat Big Jock and that was the worst thing he could do because he had to stay there at that table until Jock had a victory over him. He was always like that: snooker; golf; bowls on the beach at Minorca where we used to go on holiday every year. The game wouldn't finish until he had won. They used to talk about Bill Shankly being like that during training at Liverpool – they were out of the same mould. They had to be winners no matter what they were playing. I still think that the car crash affected him more than he let on.

Tony McGuinness It was difficult for him to admit but I reckon that he knew after the car crash that he was never going to be one hundred per cent fit again. He had a season off, supposedly, but he was still involved to some extent. Even when he came back it was too early for him. The crash damaged him badly when added to all the wear and tear he had had as Celtic manager in the previous ten years. He took all the worries, all the responsibilities on his own shoulders.

George Stein The car crash changed a whole lot of things. There were the obvious things – he rarely, if ever, played golf after the crash. But there were other, more subtle, changes in him. It had been a miracle that he survived, and I think he really looked on it as a second chance. It was, if you like, a second life for him. And, while he still wanted to get back to the game far too quickly once his recovery started, there was a bit more caution about him. I don't think in team selections and tactics he would take the chances that he would have taken earlier.

It was a terrible time for him and for all of us. Yet, in the year he was out, he was so hoping that Sean Fallon, who was in charge of the team, would win something. He didn't and that was the first time since my dad had been made manager that the club hadn't won a single trophy. They were second in the League, runners up in the League Cup and reached the quarter-finals of the European Cup

Winners Cup. But after all the success this wasn't enough for Celtic, and my dad wanted to get back to see if he could keep the momentum going. He did – he won another title, but that was the last. There was also the Scottish Cup to go alongside it in the board room at Celtic Park.

Margaret McDade When John was in that car crash the news reached all of us back home on the Saturday morning. My mother just turned her face to the wall. She wouldn't speak to us; she wouldn't eat anything; she wouldn't move. She just lay there in bed looking at the wall and refusing to listen to anything we said. We had to get the family doctor in to see her before she would start to take an interest in anything at all. And that was only when he was able to convince her that John was not dead. But all the time he was seriously ill she used to think we were keeping news from her about how he was getting on. We could not go to visit him because only Jean, Ray and George were allowed in to the hospital in Dumfries to see him. She would say to us: 'You haven't been to see John – you're not telling me everything.' She seemed convinced that he was going to die and she worried about him more and more from then on whenever he was going anywhere.

Jean Stein The crash was a terribly bad time for the family. In the first few days I think we all thought that John was going to die. But he came through, and then, after all of that, he was itching to get back. He couldn't be at peace, and yet that ankle, the same one he had hurt as a player, had been damaged again. The limp he had became worse and the ankle bothered him all the time. He had to have an operation on it again in Manchester.

George There were problems which Celtic still wanted to hand to him even when he was ill. I can remember messages coming to him while he was still in intensive care. But at that time, for the only time in his life, he just didn't want to be bothered with anything other than his own problems of getting fit again. Once that was achieved then he began to think about Celtic and to plan for the future

– but things were changing. It seemed sometimes as if all the titles and all the cups had been won by some other manager and that he was being judged season by season. I think he knew that, and winning the League and Cup double the year after the crash, the year he went back to work, helped him say to people: 'I can still do it.' But I still don't know why he had to keep proving himself.

Ray Stein I think there were times when he was in that hospital in Dumfries when we all thought he was going to die. But he had such strength and probably such a love of life that he fought back. I think it did affect him – most men his age would not have been able to go back to such a demanding job. But he did. And he went back to win another championship. It was as if he was defying the crash and whatever damage it did to him.

Jean It was sad the way things finished up at Celtic Park, and I know how badly hurt John was. I was sitting waiting outside in the car with Lady Kelly when John was talking with the directors about what was going to happen at Celtic Park. He knew that Billy McNeill was to come back, and I think he thought that would be a good thing for the club. But what was going to happen to him was different again.

When he came out he got into the car and he said: 'You'll never guess what they want me to do.' Neither of us had the slightest idea; I think we had expected that he would be general manager or something of that nature. He said: 'They want me to sell the Pools tickets!' The way he said that told us how he felt, and I couldn't believe that they would do this to him after all he had done for the club, for them. Then he kind of smiled and said that they also wanted him to be a director, that this was a suggestion. It was never more than that. Funnily enough, Lady Kelly, who knows more about Celtic Football Club than almost anyone, told him it would not happen. She was quite straight about it. She just said there and then that John would never get a seat on the board. She was absolutely right.

Ray That weekend, the weekend the story broke in the newspapers and we knew that everyone would be looking for my dad, we all took off and went down to Blackpool. We wanted to get out of the way altogether and, maybe to some extent, leave them all to it. That whole business, the way it was all handled, hurt my dad to the bone. To some extent it broke him. It was awful to know that he was suffering so much. But he could always put a face on things, and he had to do it then. It was like someone close to him dying, or even like something dying inside him. Eventually he got over it a bit.

At the time I think I realised that there were things which must have been going on in the board room before all of this had happened, but my dad would never say. He would keep that to himself because he would never want Celtic to be hurt. He would cover up anything which might have been wrong in the club and take it on his own shoulders rather than have Celtic damaged. He genuinely loved the club, not the board, but the club, and the players, and the supporters too. In the end I just think it broke him.

George When he left Celtic it was a sad, sad business. Sad for my dad and sadder for the people who had decided to get rid of him. I don't think he ever expected anything from the people who ran the club, from the directors. He maybe hoped for something. Some job he could do for the club and still help them. But *commercial manager*?

That was shocking. He looked on that as an insult. The fact that these people offered him something like that showed they didn't know the kind of man they were dealing with. Or, if they did, then they knew this was the way to get rid of him.

I still think he should have been a lot harder with those people at that time. He should have stood up more for himself, and for what he wanted. Quite honestly he just didn't think it worthwhile arguing with the type of people who thought he would make a pools agent, possibly a glorified pools agent, but none the less a pools agent. He didn't want to dignify people like that by fighting with them. If Sir Robert Kelly had been alive he would probably have become a director. But there was no way he was ever going to take the job they wanted to give him; it was demeaning. It was as if all he had done for Celtic had been forgotten after one bad season. And these were people who had not done a fraction of what he had done for the club.

Lawrie McMenemy What puzzled so many of us in the game was Celtic's reluctance to make him an offer he couldn't refuse to stay north of the border. I would have thought they would have rebuilt Hadrian's Wall just to keep him there. It was a shabby episode which led to him going to Leeds United for that short spell and then, thankfully, there was a happy ending when he went back to the Scotland team manager's job. That just about made up for the hurt he genuinely felt at being so ignored by Celtic at the end. At best, what Celtic did to the man who had made the club was insensitive.

He should at least have been offered the managing directorship at Celtic Park. His pride would not have been scarred as it was when he was offered a job selling pools tickets – and any new manager would have had the unrivalled chance of tapping the greatest of football minds. There is a lot of religion and politics mixed up in Scottish soccer, and Big Jock was always the man who could transcend all of that – until maybe at the end of his Celtic career.

Tony McGuinness Leaving Celtic broke his heart. Not losing the manager's job, because maybe he expected that to happen after the car crash and all of that. I think he probably recognised that a younger man was the answer for the manager's job – but he believed that he could still make a contribution to the playing side of things. He could have stayed there in an advisory capacity, or he could have been going out to look at players, or even helped to bring on youngsters. He would have done anything at all – just so long as it had to do with the game. The offer of a job with the Celtic Pools was an insult, and he recognised it as such. Taking him away from football was like cutting off his leg. When that offer was made it meant that he was being forced to leave Celtic, and Celtic was his life.

There was talk at the time about the Big Man being made a director – but he told me that's all it was, talk! The *Celtic View*, the official club newspaper, even said he had joined the board. Not true. Personally I think he would have been an admirable director, but not everyone thought so. According to Jock himself there was one member of the board who said that it would be 'over his dead body' if Jock Stein was ever going to be made a director of the club. I can only presume that was jealousy talking. He always ruffled a few feathers because he did not suffer fools gladly and he didn't allow directors to interfere in any way at all with team matters. That caused friction at times, and maybe it had a bit to do with what happened that summer of 1978.

Jimmy Flax It was the worst day in Celtic's history, the day that Big Jock walked out of that door for the last time! I was shattered when he left, and so were thousands of ordinary Celtic supporters. People had grown up following the team and had never known anything but that he was there as the manager – and that the team was successful. I could not believe it was possible that he would leave Celtic. He never talked much about it because it hurt too much. It has to be on some consciences that the greatest Celtic manager ever left the way he did. He spent his whole time there at the Park – he was in there night and day. He used to be there clearing the snow off the pitch if that had to be done on a Saturday morning. Sunday and all he was there, every day of the week. And every hour he was needed.

Tony Queen That Celtic mob – I don't know, I just don't. He's down in history; nine-in-a-row; the European Cup.

Bill Shankly told him in the dressing room in Lisbon: 'John, you're immortal' – that's what he said. Then they let him leave the way they did. Imagine them thinking that he would take a job looking after the pools. It was a joke, a sick joke. He is still God among the fans. They know what he did for the club even if the directors didn't. When he told me what they had offered him I could not believe it.

John Clark He never really wanted to be anywhere other than at Celtic Park. That's why he was so hurt when Billy McNeill came back as manager in 1978 and I came with him as his assistant. I don't know what happened inside the club. All I know is that we were asked to go back and I don't feel it was anything to do with Billy or myself. I never did ask Big Jock about it. But if you ask me how I felt about the Big Man being commercial manager then the answer is pretty clear. Whoever had that idea had not put a lot of thought into it. A man of his standing and achievements being pushed into that job was simply not on. I would have been happy to have had him still there, and I'm sure Billy would have been the same. OK, Billy wanted his own identity, and there might have been personality clashes, but that kind of thing happens and blows over. Big Jock would have been happy going down to England to look at players for the club or whatever – as long as it had to do with football. To be able to draw on all of his experience would have been good for us. I would have been delighted if he had stayed on and his knowledge had been available for us. Then, five years later, it happened to Billy and myself. Separately, really. Big Jock was on holiday when the end came for me, and he was in touch immediately, and from then on I seemed to get closer and closer to him.

Jimmy Reid I wish, I truly wish, that when it came time for Jock to leave Celtic Football Club, it had all been handled differently. In my opinion, and in the opinion of people who were very much closer to Jock than I was, he would have happily settled to end his days at Parkhead. But it would have to have been in some position which was commensurate with his achievements – perhaps as an honorary president of the club. Something of that nature would have been essential.

I think he was only too aware of the lack of dignity which was evident in the whole sorry affair. I never went into this at any depth with him, and I know that pictures can be misleading, but there was one photograph taken of the handover of power and there is almost a pathos in that picture. There's a look on Jock's face which says more than any words could ever say. . . .

Quite frankly, he deserved a whole lot better. But having said all of that, the events didn't diminish Jock to the slightest extent. By that time his stature was such that the negative effects were elsewhere. He behaved with that quiet dignity you would always have expected from him. That, though, was always the measure of the man. Lesser people weren't able to damage his reputation. They could hurt him, and on this occasion he was hurt, but his reputation remained intact. And his record, of course, is untouchable!

Sean Fallon Jock would never have left Celtic in the circumstances he did if Bob Kelly had still been alive. It would not have been allowed to happen that way. First and foremost the old chairman was a gentleman, and loyalty was always a priority with him. He would have stayed loyal to Jock and he would have seen that as being in the best interests of the club in any case. It is unbelievable to me even now that they thought they could do without him, without a man of his knowledge and experience – British and European. There was never going to be anyone who was going to get the better of him, yet they decided that he should be looking after the pools. I had gone myself by this time, when it happened to Jock, and I had known it was coming for me because there were a lot of things I didn't agree with which were happening at the Park. After old Bob died it was never the same – and

I think that the Big Man felt that way too. I may be wrong but I felt we had all lost something, and Jock was closer to him than anyone, so his loss was greater. I know there was talk about Jock going on the board but that never happened, and he didn't expect it to happen. All they wanted from him was that he get the pools going. Someone like him doing that sort of job! He wasn't wanted for anything else and that's where they hurt him most of all. There was no place for him on the football side of things and that had been his whole life.

Tony McGuinness We used to go down south a lot together when Jock was Scotland manager and he was looking at players there. At Liverpool he would see Bob Paisley still there, still a part of things, although he was no longer the team manager, and he would say to me: 'I could be doing that kind of job for Celtic.' Bob was there, out front for the club, giving that solid look which football people like to see. And Bob helped Liverpool in other ways, looking at players or whatever they asked him to do. Jock was never given that chance.

Yet he would have helped the club. When he went to places like Anfield or Old Trafford the red carpet went down for him. It was the kind of treatment which made you realise how highly regarded he was right through British football – and beyond. You could not have had a better ambassador, or one as widely respected. Celtic lost that.

Ray I think it's right to say that my dad was disappointed in Billy McNeill. After all, he had been the captain in all the good years, all the successful years when my dad had been in charge. My dad would have been happy enough to step down, stay in the background and be there if Billy needed advice. After he left Celtic, and probably before as well, a lot of managers did phone him and ask for help. Billy did it himself – and that guidance or advice or whatever you want to call it could have been there all the time.

George I still don't understand Billy McNeill's attitude. My dad recognised the need for a younger man to take over as manager because by that stage of his life the day-to-day involvement was becoming too much for him to handle. My understanding is that he raised the question with the directors initially. He may even have suggested Billy McNeill coming back. He was the obvious choice after his years with the club as a player, and then he had the managerial experience with Clyde and Aberdeen.

Of course, he and Billy had had a strong relationship as captain and manager earlier when Billy was a youngster at the club and my dad was the coach. They went back something like twenty years together. There had always seemed to be a special bond between them, and when Billy wanted to return to the game as manager my dad recommended him to Clyde. Then things changed and I still don't understand why. Their relationship was never the same after that – though when Billy had his own troubles at the Park, with the same people who were in charge when my dad was leaving, he rang looking for advice. My dad gave him it too and spoke to Manchester City on Billy's behalf.

If Sir Robert Kelly had been there none of it would have happened. I just don't think the people there knew anything about loyalty. There was an unwillingness at Celtic Park to recognise real loyalty.

I always had the feeling that he would have liked the kind of job that Mr McGrory had when my dad went back as manager, with maybe just a little bit more to do. Possibly the same kind of job as Willie Waddell, his old rival, had been given with Rangers – a general manager.

John Clark When he used to talk about finishing up with Celtic he would say that the thing which hurt him most was the title they offered him – commercial manager. More than anything else that hurt Big Jock. It was a slap in the face for him. If they had wanted to make him general manager then he would never have gone, and if that job had been offered to him in the later years then I'm certain he would have given up the Scotland job to go back. His heart was still at the Park, probably because he had helped create an identity for the club. He and Sir Robert Kelly did that as a partnership. There was a certain dignity about the club when they were there together.

Jean By the time he was offered that job by Celtic I think he knew the type of people he was dealing with. The club had changed since Sir Robert's death and he was never as happy as he had been before. I don't think he was prepared for what they eventually offered him – but he didn't expect any favours from them.

There had been earlier signs from the board that he shouldn't look for anything from them. There was the time he won the court case after the car crash. It took a long time, but eventually John won a settlement from the driver who had been at fault in the accident. When that settlement was finalised the club, Celtic Football Club, took back the wages they had given him for that year when he was sick. He was off for the whole season, more or less, and the only thing he did was to be there to help Sean once he was feeling fitter. The club had paid him his basic salary as normal, and then they took it back. I never trusted them after that and I don't think John did either. He couldn't believe it had happened to him.

Gerry Woolard It was a terrible blow to him when he left Celtic, you know. He did not expect that kind of treatment from them even though he had been disappointed by their attitudes on other matters. After the board told him that they wanted him to sell pools tickets for the club, he came to me for advice.

I will never forget him that day. I've never seen him so badly affected by anything. He was shattered, totally and absolutely devastated. Celtic did nothing wrong legally. They could offer him any job they wanted to. But the morality of the whole business left a lot to be desired. If Sir Robert Kelly had still been alive then it would never have happened. John had had a magnificent rapport with Sir Robert. He would never have asked the Big Man to go out and be a ticket salesman, not after all the years he had spent as manager, the most successful manager they have ever had.

OK, he was making way for new blood, for a younger manager, Billy McNeill – that he could accept. But not the job they offered him. He had taken over the job from Jimmy McGrory all those years before and Mr McGrory had stayed on as general manager and John continued to call him 'Boss' because he had that kind of respect for him. I think he would have appreciated the same kind of treatment and the chance to retain his dignity and also his interest in the game. He would have been happy scouting, just being there and being involved in the football side of things. He didn't want to sell lottery tickets.

In my view, which is based on what John told me at the time and later, the board was totally to blame for mishandling the situation. Billy McNeill wanted the job and that was only natural, any young manager with ambition would have wanted it. But I think because of the way things happened the relationship between John and Billy was soured for quite a spell. Latterly, though, Billy was asking for advice, especially when he had his own troubles with the Celtic directors. And John gave him advice. Good advice too, I'm certain, because there was no one wiser in the ways of football than he was.

It was in other areas that he was naïve – and I discovered that when he asked me to take over his financial affairs.

Some of the silverware at Celtic Park which Jock Stein brought to the club so regularly

Jock and Jean Stein outside Buckingham Palace after he had been awarded the C.B.E.

Graeme Souness, Stein's Scotland captain, in a clash with England

Hampden sees a line-up of Scotland's backroom men – Stein with Celtic and Scotland masseur Jimmy Steel and his then assistant manager Jim McLean of Dundee United

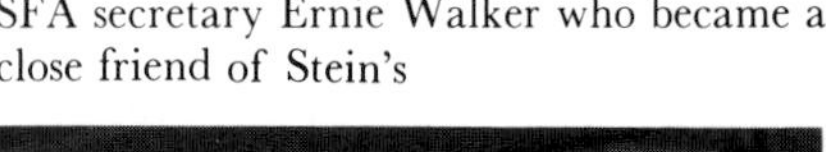

SFA secretary Ernie Walker who became a close friend of Stein's

Scotland training session with Charlie Nicholas, John Wark and Andy Gray

With Neville Southall before Scotland's 1-1 draw with Wales. After the match came Stein's tragic death

A qualifying game in Seville against Spain and Jock Stein talks things over with a worried looking Alex Ferguson, now the Manchester United manager, but then boss of Aberdeen and Stein's right-hand man with Scotland

Pat Crerand, Celtic and Manchester United

Lawrie McMenemy

8
The price of loyalty

Over the years with Celtic, Jock Stein was tempted by several job offers. He was asked to take over Coventry City after Jimmy Hill left, and at a time when Coventry were riding high. . . . He was offered the manager's job at Manchester United, and that came closest of all to luring him from his beloved Celtic. . . . And there were several approaches made for him to take over the Scotland international team manager's job, particularly after he had tasted that position temporarily in the run-up to the World Cup Finals in England in 1966.

But it was only after Celtic had peremptorily cast Stein aside that he did leave. And he went to Leeds United, which had once been ruled by his old friend Don Revie.

There were always suggestions that Stein was so highly rewarded by Celtic that he would have lost financially on any deal which would have taken him away from the club. This was not true. Stein could have been a far wealthier man if he had taken *any* of the jobs which were offered to him. He stayed with Celtic because of a stubborn loyalty – but the price in financial terms was high.

Gerry Woolard John Stein was not a money-conscious man, never mind what people say, or what they have said in the past. The man had no idea at all about financial situations. Basically he did not handle money all that well, because money as such was not important to him. Until his health began to cause him concern he did not care overmuch. It was only when he worried about illness that he wanted to make sure everything was in order. It was not money which kept him at Celtic for all these years. It was just straight, unadulterated loyalty.

Lawrie McMenemy Jock Stein could have commanded any kind of salary he wanted in England. There is no doubt that if he had moved south and had a fraction of the success he had with Celtic he would have been very handsomely rewarded. And he would have had that success, don't ever doubt that.

George Stein I can never remember him worrying about money or about his salary because basically doing the job at Celtic and being manager there meant more to him than whatever salary he was being paid. It was only later when he moved that he realised he could have – and should have – been making so much more.

But that side of things simply didn't concern him. When the offer came from Manchester United I wanted him to take it. I really did. By then I thought he had genuinely achieved everything it was possible for him to achieve with Celtic. But there were several things which went against the move. . . .

He knew that my mum was totally opposed to the move. She wanted to stay in Scotland, and even though Manchester wasn't all that far away she just didn't want to leave her home, her family and her friends. That weighed heavily with him, just as it was to do again when the Leeds United job came up all those years later.

Also, the Celtic chairman Sir Robert Kelly was ill at that time and he felt a strong sense of personal loyalty to the chairman as well as to the club. It was almost a sense of gratitude he had because they had brought him back from Wales and given him success as a player. He had that kind of sentimental streak in his make up although he would try to hide it.

And Celtic were heading for another title, the sixth in a row I think it was, and he had the European Cup and that challenge looming ahead of him again.

He had an additional worry – the influence that Sir Matt Busby might still exert over the playing side of things.

I was there when he was officially given the offer of the job by Sir Matt. Or, at least, I was a witness to it all. They met secretly after we had been to see Liverpool play in a game at Anfield. We stopped at this petrol station just before going on to the motorway north, and a few minutes later Sir Matt pulled in too and my dad went to his car and talked things over for about three-quarters of an hour. I was the 'wee boy' watching it all – not so 'wee' really, I was about sixteen – and knowing that I was watching football history in the making. All the way home he talked about the offer which had been made and initially I was sure that he was ready to accept. He loved Old Trafford of course, and all the glamour which surrounded the place. There was always a fantastic atmosphere at games there, and it was without any doubt the biggest club job available. I think it still is. So that had a big influence on his thinking.

Gradually, though, the more he talked the more the doubts filtered through. Not about my mum's feelings, because he knew that she was reluctant to move, but about the job itself. He had always insisted in every job he had that he was in complete control of the playing side. He would not take a job under any other circumstances. Basically he wondered if he would be allowed to be his own man. He was insisting that he wanted to bring in his own backroom staff so that he had his own people round about him. But Sir Matt had his own loyalties, and he wanted this one kept on and the next one kept on, and he was suggesting that maybe this bit of business should be handled in this way, and so on. The conversation in that car at the petrol station went through all of this. Dad did want Sir Matt to be there. He knew that he would need to have him around the place when he needed advice about the club – but he wanted to be his own man and he agonised over whether that would be possible or not.

Ray Stein Even with the problems which might have surrounded the job itself, George and I wanted him to go to Manchester United. It just seemed to be the right job for him. George had been accepted at college in Manchester, the club was one my dad always talked about, and I thought that it was time for him to leave Celtic. He stayed too long with the club, and at the end of it all he got his thanks! Something died in him when he left Celtic at the end, but he should have gone earlier. When the blow came and he sat down and thought back over things I think he regretted not taking the Manchester United job. He would have loved it. The worst thing that ever happened wasn't the way he was treated at the end – it was staying there too long so he could be treated that way. I remember arguing with him about that, about being so loyal to the club. He was angry when Kenny Dalglish wanted to leave Celtic, and he had been angry earlier when Davie Hay had left – though he admitted later that Kenny, in particular, had been right. But he didn't see that there was anything better than Celtic. It was much later before he learned that for himself.

Jean Stein He didn't go to Manchester United because of me. I was against it. I didn't want to go to Manchester to live because Ray was just getting married at that time and it seemed we would be so far away from her and the rest of the family. She wanted us to go, and George wanted to go as he was going to go to university there, and John wanted to go because I think he would have liked to be there at Old Trafford. Now, thinking about it, maybe I was stupid.

The way things finished up with Celtic, maybe he should have gone to Old Trafford. But, you see, I thought that he would have been at Celtic Park for the rest of his days and it didn't work out that way. It didn't work out that way for him at all.

He talked about it all with Sir Robert. The Chairman was ill at the time, mind you. But I used to tell him it's better with the devil you know than the one you don't – so just stay with Celtic. He could have made a lot more money if he had gone to Manchester United. There's no doubting that, but money was never John's god.

He loved the thought of going to Manchester United, and I know that he thought he would be successful there. There was no reason to suppose otherwise. He had been successful everywhere else and he had a great respect for Sir Matt. But I didn't think it was right, and so he stayed.

Pat Crerand I was the go-between when Jock was offered the Manchester United job, and I can still remember how it all came about. I'll never forget it. For a little while Matt had been talking about retiring. He thought he had gone on long enough in the job and he kept bringing up the subject when we were all together.

One day he raised it, and I said, why don't you approach Jock Stein? Because, to me, the two of them were so alike in so many ways that Jock was the logical man to be his successor. Both of them were lovely men and both came from that Lanarkshire mining background. It seemed a natural choice and I wondered why Matt had not thought about Jock already. The problem had been, apparently, that Matt was certain that Jock would have a contract with Celtic that would rule him out.

I told him that I doubted very much if Jock did have any kind of contract because Celtic were not a club known to give contracts to their managers. So when he heard my views on it he sent me up to Glasgow to try to sound out Jock about his taking over the job at Old Trafford. I went up to see Celtic play Ajax at Hampden in a European Cup quarter-final. They had lost 3–0 in the first leg, and while they won 1–0 they were knocked out of the tournament and, to be honest, I didn't get a chance to get near Jock at the ground. I knew how he would be feeling after that result in any case. Outside, though, I met Tony Queen, who had been a good friend to me all through my career as well as being Big Jock's closest pal in Glasgow. Tony and his wife Bunty were going over to Jock's house after the game. At the time the Big Man lived very close to Hampden and Tony asked me to come over with them and say hello.

That was the chance to speak to Jock on his own that I wanted. I went along and Bob Shankly and his wife were in the house too. Obviously Jock was down after losing, but we started to chat away about the game and then he told me to go upstairs to see his son. Young George was in bed; I knew that he was pro-United. He loved going to Old Trafford with his dad and he loved Denis Law, and so while I was talking to him I decided to tell him the reason behind my visit. I remember telling him: 'I'm here to ask your dad to go to Old Trafford' – and I can remember his reaction. He wanted that job for his dad. It was the same when Ray, his daughter, came in. I told her and there were the three of us sitting upstairs with that secret and I hadn't told Big Jock yet. Eventually he came upstairs and I told him that Matt wanted him to become the next manager of Manchester United.

He was excited at the thought – you could see that. He confirmed that there was no contract with Celtic and there would be no barriers in that sense to any move. We must have sat up there talking for a long, long time, and I can remember that Jean took the needle because she still had people downstairs and there we were all sitting and ignoring them. So I told her, too, what it was all about. And straightaway she told me: 'I don't want to go. I'm a Celtic supporter and I just want to stay up here.'

Anyway, I went back to Manchester and told Matt, and from then on I left it alone. Any other talks had to be at a higher level, but I was sure that Jock would take the job, and obviously I was hoping that he would. I'd told Jean that it was the biggest club in Europe who wanted him and I hoped that would persuade her that the move was right for all of them. I knew it was the right one for them – just as I knew it was the right one for United!

So Jock came down and I think he met Matt and Louis Edwards, who was the club chairman at the chairman's house at Alderley Edge. I guessed that progress was being made. Then Jock came down to see a Fairs Cup tie between Liverpool and Leeds, and afterwards he met Matt. Young George was there too and that was the meeting where Matt thought the job was clinched.

He told me as much, and then twenty-four hours later we were going to London to play Chelsea, and as he got on the train he turned and said to me: 'Some pal you've got.' Jock had phoned him that morning to say he was staying at Parkhead.

Matt has always maintained that Jock shook hands with him on the deal, that he was taking the job as manager of United. And I think maybe Matt thought Jock had used the offer to get more money from Celtic. That was only because of his disappointment, I reckon, at not getting him. Jock didn't do that – he simply realised that Jean was not going to move. She didn't want to come south and he couldn't change her mind.

It was a blow to Matt, and it was a blow to me and to the whole club as well. If Jock had come to United then the years of troubles and problems would never have taken place.

He was the man who would have kept United at the top. I don't have any doubts about that. He would have made them as successful as he made Celtic. In my book he was the one man in Britain who could have taken over successfully from Matt Busby. They were two of a kind.

Tony Queen I can still remember going over to Jock's house in King's Park to talk about the Manchester United job. He wanted my wife Bunty and me to go over and hear all about it and maybe sound us out a little bit on what would be best for him. But Jean didn't want to go. She was adamant. I said to her that if he was offered a better job in Hong Kong she should be ready to go there. But she wouldn't budge on it at all. She didn't want to miss Bunty and her other pals like Nancy McGraw and Leila Flynn, and the family, too, was a big consideration for her. Eventually she had the influence to change his mind. He knew that it was no use going anywhere if your wife was not going to be happy.

My advice to him was that he should go and take the job because it was meant for him. The whole set-up was so much better than the one he had been used to with Celtic, including the money, but even that couldn't tempt him away when Jean made up her mind. He used to stand up in that big guest room they have at Old Trafford and look around and admire all of it. He loved that place, he thought it was the best, and yet he turned down the job. Probably he regretted it, but I reckon Manchester United must have regretted it more down through the years. If he had gone there then they would not have had all the problems which have plagued them. He would have turned them round, and they would have continued to be at the top. I'm sure of that.

Tony McGuinness He definitely would have liked to try his luck with Manchester United. He used to talk about that a lot on the journeys up and down the motorway. He used to show me the spot where he had that secret meeting with Sir Matt Busby and was offered the job. Jean was dead set against the move, of course; Sir Robert Kelly was ill at the time, and Jock thought a lot of the chairman. Apparently he said to him: 'Do you think that Jock Stein of Manchester United sounds as good as Jock Stein of Celtic? I don't!' In that way he was telling him that he was better to stay with the club he loved above all others.

The combination of Sir Robert and Jean couldn't be beaten. That's why he stayed . . . but it was the biggest temptation he had in all the time he was with Celtic. There were other offers, but none of them caused him as much of a problem as that one.

George I can always remember Harry Hood telling me how he broke the news to the players that he was staying.

Nothing had been said officially about the Manchester United offer, but the grapevine had been buzzing and all sorts of speculation had taken place. Just around the time he was making up his mind to stay, Celtic were travelling to Aberdeen, their closest challengers for the title. They needed a draw up there at least if they were to get that sixth title in succession. They had stayed overnight at Stonehaven, and the next morning before the game he spoke to all the players: 'I want you to go out and get a result which will win us the League again – because I want to be in the European Cup next season. That's important for us all.' They drew that game – and that was enough. Twelve days later they had clinched the title.

At the time of the talk the players didn't really know that he was telling them he was staying, that he would not be going to Manchester United. That was his way of killing the rumours as far as the players were concerned. It was later on before they realised what he had been saying to them all. It was typical of him to do it in such an oblique way rather than make any big song and dance about it. Mind you, I wish he had taken the job. It would have crowned his career.

I always had the view that he should have gone to England for a spell in his managerial career. A long spell, I mean, not just the short time he had at Leeds. There were always the critics in England who suggested that Celtic had all their success only because they were the big fish in the little pond of the Scottish League. By inference they were saying the same about my dad, and it would have been good for him to go down there and compete with them and show them. He would have loved to have led Manchester United out on to Wembley for an English Cup Final. Or to win the title with them.

Jimmy Reid From the point of view of the development of his own career, Jock stayed too long with Celtic. After four or five years he had won everything. The lot. I said earlier that this might not have been good for Scottish football –

I'm not all that sure it was good for Jock either. There is no doubt in my mind that at the height of his powers Jock Stein would have been successful with any club in any country in the world. He had something which set him apart – and if it was not always recognised in Britain, it was recognised elsewhere.

I would have enjoyed seeing him in charge of a club like Manchester United. It would have been beneficial to his career and it was the type of challenge that Jock loved to take on board. He would have joined Busby in the Hall of Fame at Old Trafford – no one should seriously doubt that. It would have been the perfect stage for him.

Sean Fallon He didn't say directly at the time that Manchester United had made him an offer, but that was natural because it was his own business and he wanted to keep things quiet. All he said to me was that it was possible that he would be moving. I didn't know whether that was going to be to Old Trafford or maybe to the Scotland job. They always wanted him for that one, you know.

At the end of the day the United job was his for the taking, and maybe he should have gone. With the chairman ill there were little things happening at the club which didn't please him too much. If he had gone he would have changed things for the better at Old Trafford. Every club he was ever with he did something for. With the resources that Manchester United had then it would be difficult to see him doing any less for them. He would surely have done even more. You have to remember that at Celtic Park there was very little money spent over the years. There were a few players bought, but not all that many, and there was a lot of money made by the club over these successful years. And I mean a hell of a lot of money because you are talking about playing in the European Cup almost every year and having huge gates at Celtic Park for all the big matches. Anyway, Jock did all of what he did with Celtic and scarcely spent any of that money.

Manchester United would have given him cash to spend and he would have given them what they wanted. Success.

Jean Until the Leeds job came up I think it was only really the offer from Manchester United which tempted him. He had the chance to go to Coventry when Jimmy Hill was leaving. Jimmy Hill and one of the directors flew up and came to our house to try to persuade John. They sat in the front room and tried everything to talk him round, and I know they offered a lot of money. But it didn't mean anything to him.

Gerry Woolard The upturn in his fortunes came with the testimonial match Celtic granted him. That came after the dust had died down a little following the changes at Parkhead in that summer of 1978 – and a week before he was to take the job he had been offered by Leeds United. The proceeds from that game, the money paid by the fans to see Liverpool play Celtic at Parkhead, gave him a capital base he had never had before. Then, of course, his jobs after leaving Celtic paid him much better than he had ever known, or probably ever expected, in his years at Parkhead.

The figures I have will astonish most people. Other football managers will be shattered to realise just how poorly paid he was while he was at the very top of his profession. His salary at Celtic Park never compared with the money that people were being paid elsewhere. In England he would have commanded a salary of three or four times as much as he was getting from Celtic. That was, in fact, shown when he went to Leeds. And there were wealthier clubs than Leeds United in the First Division!

His last annual salary with the club was just £12,100 in 1977. In the previous years he had made £11,900 in 1971, when he won the League and Cup double, reached the final of the League Cup and the quarter-finals of the European Cup.

In 1972 he earned £13,000 from Celtic, when he had another double and reached the semi-finals of the European Cup; in 1973 he made his highest money ever – £16,000, and he won the title that year; in 1974 he was back down to £13,000. That year he had another League and Cup double as well as another European Cup semi-final; in 1975 he edged back up to £13,900 and he won the League Cup and the Scottish Cup; in 1976 he rose to £15,600, which was the year he missed most of the season because of the car crash and the injuries he sustained.

There are variations because everything was geared to bonuses for success either at home or in Europe. Some of the bonuses fell in a different financial year and therefore there are apparent discrepancies.

In essence I doubt very much if his actual basic salary was much beyond £10,000 a year. It never appeared to concern him too much because he never wanted to be bothered going over financial accounts. Talk football to him, fine! Do that twenty-four hours a day, seven days a week and fifty-two weeks of the year, and he was your man. But don't bother him about money.

It was only when he went to Leeds that he had his eyes opened. I think it was then that he realised that he had been a bit foolish staying on that low salary with Celtic. I don't say he would have left them, walked out on them, but he would have asked for more money if he had really known what other managers at lesser clubs were earning.

Ernie Walker Jock was never a wealthy man because, during his career, in spite of all the success, he was never well paid. And, of course, there was no pension as a manager. He used to say to me sometimes that over the years this myth had grown up that he was very highly paid as a manager – and he wasn't. As a top manager, looking at the salaries of other top managers, he was, in fact, poorly paid. When he joined the [Scottish Football] Association as team manager he virtually doubled his salary. Then a year or so later I told him he was to get an increase. I don't think he believed me at first. But we have a system in the Association whereby an independent assessment of salaries takes place annually. They recommend what kind of salary increase should be made to members of the staff and I had insisted that the team manager be included in this assessment.

While the manager was there on a contractual basis I still felt it only right that he should be covered in this way along with every other member of the staff. He didn't say anything when I mentioned the rise to him. Then, two weeks or so later, he came to me and he said: 'I've never had a rise from anyone in my life unless I have gone in to ask for one.' That was hard to believe – but I know it was true. He got a rise every year he was here with the Association. I like to think he appreciated that.

Gerry Woolard For personal happiness he made the right move when he took the job as Scotland team manager. He and Ernie Walker had a great understanding and they became very, very close. The SFA, in every sense, cared a great deal about Jock and about his family. They also paid him a much better salary than any he had earned before.

That all contributed towards making him a reasonably wealthy man when he died. Initially, when he came to us, he didn't bother about his financial condition. But with his illness he wanted to make sure everything was in order for his family.

We used to buy shares for him in various blue-chip companies – top groups really – and he would be forever checking on their progress. It was funny. He used to pore over the financial pages and then he would phone and talk to me about it. That became his gamble. He loved the horses, we all know that, but the stories about his gambling problems were wildly exaggerated.

Somehow the image Joe Public had of Jock was of a man who had gambled away his money. I don't know how all of these rumours began but it is good to know that we can quash them by hard financial facts. In 1984 his various investments gave him a profit of £29,750 – yet the street talk in Glasgow was that he was broke. Nonsense. His estate totalled £172,674.95, and that was only around sixty per cent of his total worth. He was always ready in his later years to listen to financial advice, and he would take it. In the end, that benefited his family. There was a whole load of rubbish talked about the man, and I'm glad we can put the record straight.

Tony Queen The talk about gambling and betting the horses may have had some truth in it because he liked the horses. But he never had a bet with me in his life. The rumours in Glasgow that he owed me money were nonsense. I never even discussed punting with him. If he had phoned me and suggested having a big bet with me I would have chased him – but he never did. We never talked about gambling because it was something that might have spoiled a friendship, and neither of us wanted to do that.

If he punted then I didn't know about it. He was a fairly wealthy man when he died, so how could all these stories about him be true? I'd just like one person to repeat any of these stories in front of me. They would get their answer quickly. And publicly. It's a terrible thing how people try to knock anyone who is successful. I don't know why, but it happens and they seem to wait until people die before they start up all the crazy stories. Of course, some of them were simply malicious. There were a lot of people who would have liked to be close to Jock, but he didn't give his friendship easily. Some folk resented that, but it was the way he was. He had to have people around him he could trust.

Ray It was only after he had left that he became concerned about the money he had been paid by Celtic. The big house, the flash cars, being seen in the best places did not interest him one little bit. The one thing I know about my dad is that he was never jealous of anyone else. Anyone who had all these things and made big money, well that was fine, but my dad never envied any of them.

I doubt that he envied a living soul. I think he was really happy with his life in spite of disappointments over some things. He didn't grudge anyone success; he loved seeing his own players getting on. A lot of people might have hated him because, if he didn't have any time for you, then there was no way that you would ever get into his good books. Basically he was a shy person, and wary of professional people, but he knew he had to get over that and he did. His gruff manner was not the real man. He hid a lot behind that mask.

He never changed a lot. He was always, still, a big miner from Lanarkshire. That was him and he didn't want it any other way and neither did any of us.

In the end, because he was so happy with the SFA he came to believe that the people at Celtic Park had done him a favour. He didn't think so at the time, but when the hurt wore off and he settled into the Scotland job he realized he was better off. Suddenly he was being appreciated and he was working, once again, with people he had respect for. It gave him back his own respect.

Pat Crerand Some time before the end came for Jock at Celtic I was in Glasgow for an Old Firm game. Afterwards I had dinner with several Celtic people at East Kilbride. One of them was a director of the club and I was amazed to hear him start talking about how Jock would have to be replaced as manager. I could hardly believe my ears. They were talking about the man who made the club. That's what he must have been up against. It angered me that anyone should even think that way about Big Jock.

Jean Lady Kelly told me that if Sir Robert had been alive then John would have been general manager of the club. She was in no doubt about that.

9
Forty-four days at Leeds – then back to Scotland

When the sad and undignified ending came at Celtic Park, it was Leeds United who threw the initial lifeline to Jock Stein and his managerial career.

The Elland Road club had been sinking lower and lower since the departure of Stein's old rival and friend Don Revie some years earlier. The chairman Manny Cussins and his directors approached Stein and invited him to take on the job of resurrecting the club.

The problems which had prevented the move to Manchester United all those years earlier were to surface again. Jean Stein still did not want to move from Scotland – but Stein accepted the offer and headed south.

George Stein The situation which arose at Leeds came close to splitting our family. I don't say that lightly. We have always been a very close family; everything has always been discussed and talked over, and always things were kept between us. But when my mum didn't want to go to Leeds I couldn't understand why. When Leeds had come in for him he was really happy. And those six or seven weeks there turned out to be good weeks in his life. Even when the Scotland offer arrived I was in favour of him staying at Leeds. I wanted my mum to go down there to live.

Ray Stein As George has told you, there was quite a fall-out in the family over the Leeds job. My dad did seem so happy there. He was making good money for the first time in his life; he had a club who seemed to appreciate anything he was doing for them; and he had a chairman who would have given him anything. Both George and myself wanted him to stay there. I think he did fancy taking a crack at the game in England, and rebuilding Leeds would have been good for him.

I think, too, that after what had happened at Celtic it restored his self-confidence when Leeds came in to take him south as their manager. He needed someone to show confidence in him in that way. But my mum didn't want to go, and I suppose it all worked out right in the end when the opportunity of the international job came up.

Jean Stein John knew how I felt about moving. I did go down to look at houses, but I didn't want to move to England. There was a bit of argument about it in the family because George and Ray thought he should sign a contract with Leeds, but I still wasn't keen.

Mind you, John enjoyed it down there. He liked the whole place and he liked the chairman, Manny Cussins, who would have done anything to keep John there. I did feel sorry for him when it ended. It was a blow to him because he had seen what John could do. Even in that short time, he knew that he had made the right choice. I think he saw all the good days coming back again.

Honestly, though, I didn't want to have to move south, and then, luckily, the Scotland job came up and John was approached for that and everything worked out for the best.

George He had a relationship with the chairman of Leeds United quite unlike any he had ever had before. Even better in some ways than the one he had with Sir Robert Kelly. Manny Cussins wanted success for the club, he wanted it desperately, and he genuinely believed that my dad was the man to get it for him. He was willing to pay the earth to get what he wanted. Celtic had always wanted success, but they had wanted it at as little cost to the club as possible. This was totally different, and my dad loved it.

For those few weeks he had at Elland Road he felt that he was back amongst things again, back in the big time, because Leeds were still a major club. Not the force they used to be, perhaps, but still an important club, and he was getting things going for them again. He had some good results, a couple of unlucky results, but he felt that he had the team on the right lines and he was negotiating to buy players. He had been told by the chairman that he had one-and-a-half million pounds to spend on players. That was an awful lot of money back in 1978. He was trying to buy Dave Narey from Dundee United and the Irish international Gerry Daly from, I think, Derby County. He was also negotiating for a class striker. I knew, and he knew, that if he could guide Leeds towards success again then he would be treated like a god. To get them into the top six of the First Division would have made him a hero. It was hard to grasp just how well he was being treated down there. Compared to anything that had happened in the past he was being looked after like a king. That's why I didn't want him to leave.

Ray The whole set-up at Leeds was so professional. He had to concentrate on the playing side, on the team side, and nothing else. There were less problems for him, and wee Manny Cussins just seemed thrilled to have him there as the manager. We were going down to see games and he was happy at the way things were moving.

Manny Cussins was working so hard trying to convince my mum that she would be happy at Leeds, and I think we were all trying our best to tell her that. Apart from the obvious thing of staying on his own in a hotel for most of the week, my dad was as happy as I've seen him. When he played his first game at Elland Road it was like a party. There were so many of his friends there to see how he got on and to wish him well. I think he had that whole place buzzing in a way that it hadn't been since Don Revie left.

But there is no use denying that the Scotland job was one he had wanted at various times down through the years, and when he had that chance, knowing that my mum didn't want to go to Leeds to live, then there was no choice. He came home again.

Willie Harkness The trouble was that it looked as if all the timing was out. There was Ally MacLeod resigning just a month or so after Jock had left Celtic and gone to Leeds. I felt deep down that there was only one candidate for the job and that was Jock. We needed him – especially at that time. But he had been given the job at Leeds and he was supposed to have signed a major contract.

It was then that I heard on the grapevine that, in fact, Jock had not signed any contract with Leeds. It was there, waiting for him, but he had not put his name to it. I also learned from the same person that Jock wanted to come home because his wife didn't like the idea of living in Leeds. That was all the hint I needed to get moving. I made a call to Jock at Elland Road and used another name, the name of a friend of his, so that people wouldn't start talking. I got through, spoke to him and confirmed that he did want to take over as the international team manager. From that point we arranged a meeting between myself, Jock and Tom Lauchlan, who was the chairman of the International Committee at the time and who was of the same mind as myself – that we had to get Jock into the job. We met in Dumfries, sorted everything out, and then went ahead with all the official approaches. We had to keep everything under wraps because the Leeds chairman Manny Cussins was determined to hold on to Jock at all costs. We knew this, but as there was no contract we could speak to him.

Manny wasn't too pleased when the whole deal was worked out because he so wanted to keep Jock. But I felt that he was the kind of man we needed after the shambles of Argentina. He was a kind of father figure for the whole game, someone who was respected in Scotland and all across the world for all that he had done. He restored a bit of credibility – and that's what we needed.

Maybe he wasn't as successful as he hoped he might be – but he took us to Spain and he had some very good results. It was good for me as President to know that there was someone like Jock in charge of the team. He was good for the Association and for the whole country.

Pat Crerand I can remember when the Scotland job came up. The Big Man was at Leeds, and he phoned to say that he was going over to watch Oldham play Morton in one of these Anglo–Scottish Cup games. So I went up to see him there, and on the way I heard that Ally MacLeod had left. So when I got to the ground that was the first topic of conversation. He asked me who I thought would get the job and, naturally, I said he was the only man capable of doing it. But Jock didn't think he would get the offer. It's funny, but no matter all the success he enjoyed there were still times when Jock doubted his own ability. I knew that Jean had not wanted to move south, and while he was doing well at Leeds and he was enjoying the football side of things, he was the kind of man who needed his family around him. I was glad for him when it all worked out.

Gerry Woolard No one knows this – until now. Jock Stein turned down a personal fortune to move back to Scotland and take on the team manager's job. I had been involved in the Leeds deal from the beginning. I went to Leeds with John to work out details of a contract, which was waiting to be signed when the offer came from the SFA. When it arrived officially he asked me to come to Leeds to explain the whole thing to Manny Cussins. He needed help because he knew how hurt Manny was going to be. The chairman said to him, at that meeting: 'If this is only about money then you can have all the money you want just to say here with us at Leeds United.'

It was then that he offered him a personal gift of £200,000 to stay with Leeds. This was not part of his contract, it was not to be spread over any three-year period. It was to be a personal cheque from Manny Cussins, written out there and then in favour of John Stein.

The problem was, of course, that the Big Man did not want money. He wanted to go home, and he wanted the Scotland job. He honestly believed that he could help Scotland get back to normal after all the problems in Argentina. But it was an astonishing amount of money to turn down. I would have taken it; most people would have taken it. He would have been made for life – and he turned his back on that.

He also walked away from a contract which was worth more than the SFA contract at that time. As well as the £200,000 gift, he also gave up around another £100,000 over the next three years. But he was happy, and that is what counted with him.

George I had doubts about the SFA. I didn't know how he would settle in there, and I didn't know if he would be allowed total freedom when it came to team selection and in all matters involving the playing side.

Eventually, I'm happy to say, I was proved wrong. The SFA were great for him, and he and the secretary Ernie Walker built up a tremendous relationship. The pair of them used to go off to games together, and it was ultimately a close friendship.

I think the Scotland job was good for him. But he did become more cautious than he had been with Celtic. He became more pragmatic, I suppose. He used to say to me: 'We have good players but we don't always have a good team and it's hard to get a *team* at this level.' He missed the day-to-day involvement with players, but he tried to adjust to that as much as he could.

Ray I think the SFA needed someone to stabilise things, and that was something he did. It was a good job for him in that way. The only way it wasn't so good for him was that my dad was good with people on a day-to-day basis. And because he wasn't with the players every day, he began to see things which would annoy him, things he wouldn't understand – Steve Archibald and his smoked salmon before meals; Charlie Nicholas getting a perm at Turnberry; Mo Johnston wearing ankle chains – it was these things he found harder and harder to cope with. It would have been easier to handle all that at a club. Seeing them a few times a year he had to put up with behaviour he might not have put up with as a club manager. He just didn't think some of these players' foibles were right. It was the old Lanarkshire miner peeking out again.

Maybe he wasn't the best Scotland manager, but he was the best man around at that time and it was a good job for him in spite of the growing generation gap he felt with some of the younger players.

Jean I was glad when the Scotland job did come up and I was glad that it turned out the way that it did. He was happy there and Ernie Walker became a good friend to him. I think he found the main problem in the job was the gap between seeing the players. If you had a defeat then you couldn't hammer it out in the dressing room the next day – they were all away back to their clubs. He found that difficult. He enjoyed working with Jim McLean and Alex Ferguson; he was very fond of them both. Of course, we had known Alex long before he was a manager. He used to come into a restaurant near our house in King's Park with his wife Cathie so we had known them for years and away from football.

George I think Jim McLean was a great thinker on the game, a deep thinker, and he had a good partnership with my dad. Then when Jim McLean left he was fortunate having Fergie [Alex Ferguson] there. My dad was getting older and so Fergie complemented him in that spell when they were together. He could mix with the younger players more easily, something that my dad found more and more difficult.

Also Graeme Souness was important to him, particularly after he had made Graeme his captain. He always said that when he was picking the Scotland team the name of

Souness went down on the page first. He was a natural on-field leader, and he made other people round about him play better just because of his presence. My dad recognised his professionalism and he thought the world of him.

Graeme Souness When he made me captain of Scotland I think it was a little bit of that man management he was so good at. I think he recognised me as still being a potential problem for him. It was his way of dealing with it to hand me responsibility and say 'Now live up to that!'

I can remember one incident with him in Brussels when Kenny Dalglish and I had gone shopping together. We had got our times mixed up. I said that we had to be back at the hotel at four o'clock and Kenny said that it was five o'clock. We walked in at five minutes to five and he was sitting there in reception, blue in the face. He went for me, and of course, when he was like that in full flow you couldn't say anything. You could not get a word in. Kenny was trying to say it was his fault, but he was told to shut up, and all the way to our room he gave us hell. The players along the corridor kept opening their doors to see what was going on. He went at it again in front of the rest of the players. I can remember him saying: 'Who do you two think you are that you can keep all these other players waiting? You must think you're something special.' He turned it round that little bit and we were getting it hot and strong. He was a fearsome sight when he was in that kind of mood. So by making me captain he had me as someone who was now trying to keep everyone else on time, or whatever.

He has been a big loss to me – as a person I respected and as a person I know would have helped me a lot in the job I have now. There are times when I've got problems and I know that if he had still been alive I could have picked up the phone and he would have been there with the kind of good advice he always had on offer. I can ask Bob Paisley or Joe Fagan, but he would have been different because he had experienced the game in Scotland and the

Old Firm business and he would have known exactly what I was going through. And I know he would have helped me. I like to think that I became as close as any player who had been involved on the Scottish scene with him. I liked him a lot, and I miss him.

Ernie Walker We had had our conflicts, of course, before he came into the job as team manager, and while we had a mutual respect for each other we were hardly bosom pals. He came here with many prejudices and false ideas about the SFA. His contact with the Association had usually been on a disciplinary level, and he was usually being disciplined for remarks about a referee or whatever. Jock very quickly realised that the view from in here, inside the Association, is far from being the same as the one out there among clubs and club managers. We had an early meeting after he had been appointed, and I told him that we at the Association would do everything possible to help him in his job. I stressed to him that we all understood that what brings the Association success or otherwise is the team. Jock recognised this very early on, and also began to realise that we weren't the ogres we were supposed to be.

I suppose I was as guarded about Jock as he was about me. My contact with him had been through newspaper headlines or through the tittle-tattle of football where everyone claims to know everyone else's business. I could not argue with his record, but I was worried about some of the methods he was supposed to have used to get success. I was dubious about whether he was really the straight shooter his supporters said he was. Also I didn't know whether he would fit in to our set-up. But all of that vanished very quickly when we got to know each other. He enjoyed his years here – he was happy working with the Association, and I think he regretted a little not having taken the job earlier. I certainly always felt that he should have been there earlier, from both his own and our points of view. If he had come at a relatively high point in his career it would have been so much better for him. At the end there was a sense of things disintegrating around him at Celtic Park and there was not a lot of dignity when he left there.

Ray It would have been easier for him if he had gone to the job earlier in his career. He did have a short spell as part-time manager, but that wasn't enough for him. It would have been much better if he had gone to the job as Scotland team manager when he was a few years younger. He could have gone and avoided all that wrangling at the end of his time with Celtic, for instance. I wish that had happened.

John Clark I think he did well enough with Scotland when he took on that job. But he was not the Jock Stein he was, not the Jock Stein we had back in the beginning. The accident he was involved in maybe had a bit to do with that, and also he was getting older. However, he still had that formidable presence. He was a great public relations officer for the game in Scotland as a whole. The Scotland players, sadly, got him too late. We had the best of him, and the Dunfermline and the Hibs players, too. That was the Big Man at his peak, and it's an honour to say that you worked under him then.

Lawrie McMenemy He may have been that bit older when he did get the Scotland job but his instincts were as finely tuned as ever. Physically the accident had taken its toll, but that mind was working as shrewdly as ever. He was so good at the little things, which were also the important things. I remember going up to Sotogrande on the Costa del Sol where Scotland were based for the 1982 World Cup. Jock made me very welcome as he always did. Then he told me a typical story. He had passed out menus for the players and told them he recommended they had a choice of soup or prawn cocktail to start with, then fish or meat for the main course and fruit cocktail to finish. Then he added that if any player wanted anything different just to ask.

Only one wanted something else – Steve Archibald. He

requested smoked salmon to start. That little thing told Jock a lot. It isolated Steve as a loner in a team situation. And basically, of course, Jock couldn't understand why people would want to eat differently from the way they ate at home just because they happened to be travelling with Scotland. He had all these little things he would do which would give him background on players and on how he would expect them to behave in certain circumstances. His man-management techniques were magnificent. He brought a professionalism to the Scotland scene – he brought that professionalism with him everywhere he went. No one was better than he was. And I think that the Association realised how valuable he had been for them.

Ernie Walker Early on, very early on in fact, we made a pact between us about the job. I told him that I didn't want any repeat of situations which had blown up in the past when managers had learned that their jobs were in jeopardy from an outside source, or that their position was placed in the spotlight because of ill-timed remarks from officials, or when people had walked out on us in midstream, so to speak. I told him that if it ever came to a time when he was going to be sacked – and that may come to anyone because it's one of the perils of the job – then he would not hear it whispered around. He would hear it up front, and he would hear it from me. Jock, for his part, said it would never come to that because if things reached that kind of stage then he would come to me and offer to step down. The deal was not discussed by committees or anything; it was a private thing, and I think it helped to relax us both and cement the relationship which was to grow over the years. From then on it happened just about every day that his head would come round that door just after midday and he would sit down and talk to me about problems he had, or anything. It was important for me having him in the office. He had so much experience, and he had really become the elder statesman of the game up here. Even in the south that was the way he was treated. He had so much maturity, so much wisdom, and I could use him as a sounding board for various ideas. This can be quite a lonely chair, and it was good to have someone with so much experience to provide helpful and sensible advice.

Alex Ferguson It was an education to work with Jock Stein. Jim McLean had been doing the job before me, and when he gave it up Jock offered me the chance of working with him. It was a tremendous thing for me, to be with Scotland and to be there to benefit from Jock's knowledge of the game.

I was maybe a little bit fortunate that I wasn't as much in awe of him as I might have been. Going into the job as a young manager it would have been easy to be nervous in his presence, but I'd known him outside the game. We used to see each other in a restaurant in Glasgow and we would sit and talk about the game for hours, so the ice didn't need to be broken.

Basically it was easy to fit in with what he wanted from me. He couldn't take all of the training by that stage and so he would have me do that and then he would supervise and discuss the team selection with me. Not always, mind you. There would be times he would knock ideas back and forward and other times when he would simply hand me the team he had picked. He used to worry about the players. He was never a great sleeper, and so he would sit up to all hours talking about football. He loved that – and he would sit up if players were out late. He did it because he was concerned about them. But when players were in trouble he didn't believe in sending them home or making it public. He used to say to me: 'Remember the players have families. They have mothers and fathers or wives and children and they get hurt if you make any trouble public. Deal with it quietly and that's that.' And so he would take a lot on his own shoulders. He might just drop someone from the squad and then he would get stick for that but he would never give out the reasons. He would protect his players from that kind of adverse publicity as much as possible.

His knowledge of the game and his knowledge of people was unmatched. He knew everything that was going on in Scottish football – everything. You could not beat him on that, and it all stayed in his mind. He had a tremendously retentive memory. He would see players and teams and he would remember every little thing about them. You see younger managers now with clip boards and such like. Jock didn't need them – he exercised that memory of his and it always worked. He had an encyclopaedic knowledge of the game and of players.

Ernie Walker He introduced a discipline which might have been lacking in the Scotland squad under previous managers. After the trauma of Argentina he restored a degree of respectability to the whole thing. My job was to pull the Association through after those troubles – his was to pull the team and the players through. He was not without his problems there, but they were handled skilfully and strongly. It was a difficult time after Argentina and sometimes you would find players who wanted to play in an easy game at Hampden but miss out on a difficult one away from home. He worked hard to change that, and under his management we had fewer call-offs than we had had in the past.

There was a feeling that he was such a strict disciplinarian that no one would *ever* step out of line. That was not true. He didn't handle things in quite such a black-and-white way. His skill was in being able to swim against the current in shark-infested waters and survive. He didn't always say 'I'm the Boss – you do as you're told!' Some players might get away with more than others. Really he needed to employ a certain skill and cunning to keep it all together. He had to know how far he could let some players go and how hard he had to slap down others. He could be quite cruel. Several times he told me how he might handle certain situations, how he would pick a fight with one of the weaklings in the squad – and he would do this deliberately – and by doing so he would get his point over to others he might have been aiming for originally. That way, though, he would have avoided any damaging confrontation.

Tony Queen Handling men was his secret. He would have gone far in the army. I went through the ranks and got a commission and to do that you had to study man management. He would have passed that test with flying colours. He was superb at handling players. Maybe he didn't have a fancy education, but he had been at the university of adversity, the same as myself, and he would have been successful at anything he wanted to do. He handled a team full of strong personalities at Celtic and then he handled the international players with Scotland – and he did it all better than anyone else.

John Clark Sure, there were times when you hated him. When he sold me to Morton, for example, and I didn't want to go. But he thought it was best for the team and best for me and he got me a few quid and had a younger player standing by to take over. I didn't like that, and other players had moans too. That was only natural. But we had more medals than moans, most of us. He did what he thought was right for the team, then for the club, and then for the individual, and that was right.

Pat Crerand I'm sure that he was happy in the Scotland job. He liked the job and it gave him a chance to go on to an even bigger stage. I can remember in the days I played for Scotland how amateurish it all was. There was no way it would have been that way with Jock there. He knew more about the game than any man I ever met. I'm sure that he did as good a job for Scotland as anyone could have done. To some extent it's an impossible job for anyone. But players wanted to play for Jock Stein – they didn't always want to play for other managers who were there. He added stature to that job and to any job he had.

Ernie Walker Jock saw the realities and the difficulties of the job. That was important. He never allowed himself to be carried away, and he tried to make sure that the supporters didn't get caught up in any hysteria. He knew that he didn't have as many 'great players' as the public seemed to think we had. And he knew that he would never be allowed the same team-building opportunities as, say, Brazil or West Germany. He saw the pitfalls and the problems and went to work within the limitations which were imposed on him. If the chips were down then he would play defensively. He could not resist doing that if things looked really desperate for us. There was a certain element of caution in him that might not have been there earlier in his career. That was understandable. He cared quite deeply still about winning, however. He never changed that much. He wanted to win every game, and he would become very tense before matches. Immediately before a game the big, bluff exterior that he showed the world hid a very nervous man. That was something in him which never altered down through the years.

Jimmy Reid I think it would have been so much better if he had gone to the Scotland job earlier in his career. Though, having said that, I have to admit it might not have made a great deal of difference to our results. But we would have avoided the type of thing which happened in Argentina. He would never have allowed that kind of national excess.

Sometimes you can be playing against teams with three or four world-class players in their line-up. I can remember being in Seville in 1982 when we played Brazil and that was what happened that night. I don't know if Jock had one genuine world-class player available to him in his time as manager. So while Jock's managerial and tactical skills were outstanding, he was not Merlin the Magician. I think he recognised it and he did the best he could with the skills he had at his disposal.

That is how he was able to guide the team to the World Cup Finals in Spain in 1982 and then to Mexico in 1986 – because, although he died that night in Cardiff, he had succeeded in getting us into second place in the qualifying group. One very notable thing which Jock did for us in his time as team manager was to knock down a little the totally ludicrous expectations that the public have.

For reasons which have nothing to do with football, but have everything to do with history, Scotland's football team is fastened to stupidly high expectations. The punters believe that we are serious contenders for every World Cup which is played. Qualifying for the Finals with the frequency we have done should be enough – for our fans it isn't. They look for us to go on and win the World Cup, and I don't believe that is on. And I don't think Jock ever believed it. So he scaled down these dreams and he looked at it realistically, and in so doing he brought back some dignity to the international scene. When he was the manager I was always certain that even in defeat we would emerge with dignity. There would be none of the horror stories of previous days. He brought a kind of sanity back to the scene. That miner's realism, that common sense of his, brought us down from the clouds. And we all needed it. That was the job he did.

10
The last hurrah

On 10 September, 1985, the Scottish supporters streamed into Cardiff ready to see their team qualify for the World Cup Finals for the fourth time in succession. When they left that night they had seen their team get the vital point they needed – but most of them didn't care.

For Jock Stein, the legend who had led them so far, had died that night at Ninian Park. It was a tragic end to the career of a man who had dominated Scottish soccer for the best part of three decades.

Jean Stein I knew John was ill, of course, but none of us realised how ill. He was not the type of man who appreciated people making a fuss, but there had been a warning that the strain was sometimes getting to be too much.

After the Welsh game at Hampden he took a bad turn in the house. He had been keyed up for that game, a win then and Scotland would just about have qualified for the Finals. The team lost 1–0 and he took it badly. At home watching the game again on the television he wasn't well at all and he had to take pills for his heart condition. It worried me, but he shrugged it off when the pain went away. He said that all he needed were the pills – but looking back I think he might have had a slight heart attack that night. He was not a man for taking warnings. He wanted to qualify again so much that nothing would have stopped him.

Ray Stein The first game against Wales disappointed my dad a lot. I think he had built up his hopes after the good

With grandson John in a special garden training session

At the World Cup draw for the Finals in Spain along with Britain's other managers taking part – Billy Bingham of Northern Ireland and Ron Greenwood of England

On the beach in Portugal – but not on holiday. One of the few brief moments of relaxation before the beginning of the World Cup in Spain in 1982

Stein on the training ground at a Scotland team work-out

David Narey scores for Scotland against Brazil, in the 1982 World Cup Finals

Steve Archibald tussles with Cerezo in the same match

At home with Jock and Jean Stein and grandson John

Grandson John, at rear, granddaughter Stefanie and the grandson Jock never saw, Jonathan – the new 'Jon' Stein

results the team had had before that, and he was convinced that we would make sure of qualification early. When it didn't happen he had a bad turn at home and maybe then we should have known that the pressure was building on him. But he never gave us the slightest clue that anything was wrong. It was only after what happened at Cardiff that we learned about little things he had done and we realised that he had behaved a little bit differently before leaving. But on their own these things meant nothing. It was only afterwards that we put it all together and saw some kind of pattern which suggested that he knew that he was not well.

George Stein I was in Switzerland that night. I watched the game, and when the cameras switched to the bench I could see he was not right. He was just sitting there, showing no emotion. In hindsight you wonder if something could have been done – but that's wrong. He would not have allowed anything to be done.

Alex Ferguson told me that he seemed confused at half time – but there was confusion in the dressing room because of the way the game was going. Fergie sometimes blames himself for not noticing that he wasn't well, but if he had seen anything and said something then he would have got a blast and would have been told to watch the game. That's just the way my dad was.

When we lost to Wales in the first match my mum thinks he had a mild heart attack that night at home. He had picked up a virus in Spain, too, and he never shook that off. Then, after the Welsh game at Hampden, nothing seemed to go right. He went in for an operation, and while new technology suggests it was a minor operation I thought it drained him of a lot of his strength. He came to Switzerland that summer and rarely went out. He just seemed so tired – that was the last time I saw him.

Ray He had a cough that wouldn't go away and he wasn't his usual bouncy self. He used to come round to the house in the afternoons and he would just sit there and watch the telly, usually the racing if it was on. It was funny but he didn't want any of us to go to that game in Wales. There was no way that I was to be allowed to go down to that match, and yet usually he liked us all to be around. He liked us to put in an appearance, so to speak. He didn't want George there either, even though he was trying to get a flight over. I told George that it would only upset my dad and so he stayed in Switzerland. I picked my dad up the night he was going away. He was going to the Excelsior Hotel at Glasgow Airport, and he looked unwell. He was feeling the pressure, and I think he knew that we would all feel it too if we went to the game. He was trying to save us some of that.

There were some things which happened that give you a funny feeling now when you look back. Just wee things he did. But I never thought he was going to die.

Jean We were in the house that Saturday night when Ray came to pick him up and he kissed me goodbye – and that was something he would never normally do in front of people. John wasn't like that, he wasn't demonstrative. And then, on the morning of the game, he phoned me at home for a chat. Again, that was a change from the usual routine. On match days he never phoned because he was always so wrapped up in what he was doing, and I understood that. It's funny when you think about these things now.

Ernie Walker The night that Wales beat us at Hampden – I think Jock was feeling the illness from then on. He never seemed himself after that. If we had not lost that game at Hampden, maybe he would still have been with us today. It placed a terrible strain on him. No matter how he spent his summer, he knew – as we all knew – that there was the awful spectre of going to Wales and perhaps failing to qualify. It was a dreadful thought because now the Scottish supporters expect the team to be in the Finals every four years.

One of the secretaries in the Association, Marjory

Nimmo, handled all Jock's administrative work for him. She looked after letters and all the rest of the things he had to attend to. Now that was not his forte – administration. He didn't enjoy it, and it was a chore to him. Yet before he went to Wales he put all of his papers in order. Everything had been dealt with. It was as if he anticipated that something was going to happen to him. A recognition that he was not very well. Maybe even that he felt he was going to die. It was strange.

Alex Ferguson I look back and wonder all the time if I might have been able to do something to help the man. There was a lot of confusion in the dressing room about substitutions in the second half and so on, and he wasn't as much in command as usual; he just sat there. But I was upset because Jim Leighton had lost a contact lens and I didn't even know that he wore them. I felt that he had embarrassed me in front of Big Jock because I should have known that about one of my own players. So that was occupying me, and then in the second half, after we scored from the penalty to equalise, I jumped up, and when I sat down again I can remember patting him on the head and saying: 'That's it, we've done it, we're there.' But he was subdued, and all he kept saying was 'Keep your dignity at the end. No matter what happens, keep your dignity. Keep the players on the park and let them go to our supporters before they come in.' He kept going on about this, and at the end when he collapsed I had to keep the players out there. It was almost prophetic. He got up to go – that was what he used to do, get up the tunnel right on the final whistle. He said, 'I'm away,' and then he staggered, and Hugh Allan the trainer jumped up to grab him, and then other people took him inside. We didn't think it was as bad as it all turned out to be. Not then, not immediately. A little later I was even told he was OK.

Graeme Souness I was coming out of the stand when I bumped into Ernie Walker; there were several minutes to go. It was after the penalty. I was in the stand because, although I was suspended for that match, Big Jock had asked me to join the squad because I was captain.

In the dressing room at half time he said to me, 'What shall we do?' That wasn't him. He *always* knew what to do. He didn't ask anyone. That was the first time I had seen him not in control of a dressing-room situation. It was strange. I remember when he came to Italy to see me. He was relaxed, and he had been such great company. I think that got me closer to him, so the loss I felt was enormous. I could not believe it when it happened. I saw it on one of the television monitors upstairs at Ninian Park and ran down to see if there was anything I could do. There wasn't, of course. It was up to the doctor by then. I waited outside the treatment-room door.

Ernie Walker The older I get the worse it becomes for me to sit through really tense games, and it was that way that night at Cardiff. I could not sit in my seat after the penalty goal we scored and I went out of the directors' box and downstairs to the board room. I met Graeme Souness on the landing and he seemed to be in as bad a state as I was. I went into the inner sanctum there to pour him and myself a drink. I didn't even want to watch the monitors, but Graeme went out and he saw what happened and rushed downstairs to the dressing-room area. I found out the game was over and I pushed my way through to the room where he was being treated. The Association treasurer Bill Dickie, the doctor Stewart Hillis, myself and a Welsh official were the only people there. He seemed to be in pain and maybe in shock but he spoke to me. He said either 'I'm all right, Ernie', or 'It's all right, Ernie.' It still troubles me to this day that I don't know exactly what he said to me. Then he kept saying, 'It's this bloody cough' – the cough which had been bothering him for many months. The ambulance men arrived with resuscitation equipment, and we thought he was going to be OK. It looked as if the crisis had passed – and then he died. The little monitor screens told us all that. Nothing mattered to me after that. It didn't matter that we had qualified. It was the end of a man's life, the end of a career, the end of so many things, because he had dominated the game for so long. I lost a friend – but the game lost much more. Mexico didn't matter.

Alex Ferguson The first news I got was that he was going to be all right. I told the players that in the dressing room, and it just seemed that everything was fine. Jock was OK, we had got through, and we were surely heading for the Finals. It was great. Then I went out of the dressing room and I saw Graeme Souness standing at the treatment room, and he was crying. He told me: 'The Gaffer's struggling,' and then minutes later we heard he was dead. It didn't seem possible.

Jessie McNeill When it happened, Margaret and I were on our knees in the kitchen praying. We thought that perhaps he had stumbled going up the tunnel because he liked to get out of the way at the end of a game. We didn't know what had happened, so we phoned Jean, and after about ten minutes we got through and she said to us: 'John's ill, but when he takes one of his tablets he will be OK.' Then not long after that a friend of Ray's phoned to tell us he had died. We could not believe it. The shock was too much for all of us.

Ray I went round to my mum's right away. At first, of course, we thought he was going to be all right. We thought maybe it would be like the wee attack he had after the Hampden match and that his pills would clear everything up. Then we got the phone call which told us he was dead. We had to get in touch with George, and it was just awful. It was so hard to think that my dad was not coming home. I have thought and thought about it since that night and I'm sure of one thing: that it was the way in which he would have wanted to go. At least he died knowing that things had worked out right for him and the team.

Jean You know, he never saw his new grandson Jonathan. George's wife had had Jonathan just before Cardiff and we were planning to go to Switzerland to see the new baby –

the new Jon Stein I suppose, the one who will keep the name on. It was sad he never saw that wee one.

You just keep wondering if there was anything we could have done, but John would not have wanted fuss. If it had to happen then it happened the right way for him. He wouldn't have wanted to be an invalid. He would have hated that.

Lawrie McMenemy You know, before the game in Cardiff Jock told me that he reckoned Davie Cooper would be the match winner. He didn't want to play him from the start because he would be man marked, but he planned to bring him on later so the Welsh would be tired and he would be fresh. Cooper went on and he turned the game. Jock knew that Scotland were going to Mexico when he collapsed. He had always given everything he had to football – this time he gave his life.

I went to the funeral, and that said more than anything else what the ordinary people thought about Jock Stein. Mile after mile of streets were lined with ordinary men and women who simply wanted to pay their last respects. It was a very emotional day. I was crammed into a corner at the service with Rod Stewart and Graeme Souness. When I looked at Graeme, at first I thought he had a heavy cold – but in fact he was crying. He is one of the hardest men in football, yet he was not ashamed to cry that day. Like the rest of us, he knew that a great man had died.

Alex Ferguson All the time I was with him in the Scottish set-up I never once heard him talk about his achievements. I used to try to draw him during our talk sessions, but he didn't like to boast about anything. He had the kind of humility that only really great men possess. Not well-known men, genuinely great men. He was one of them.

Pat Crerand The day of the funeral was a desperate day. I had seen Jock collapse on television, and it was just so hard to accept that he was gone. He used to come to see me whenever he was down for a game, and he would come in with Scottish rolls and sausages and things that he knew

I couldn't get in Manchester. It was so difficult to realise that you wouldn't see him any more.

I'll tell you this, a hundred years from today all of us will be forgotten, no matter who we are and how important we think we are. No one will remember us. But Jock Stein will be remembered. He made Celtic, and he was the greatest manager Scotland ever produced. I'm just glad that I have such great memories of the man.

Graeme Souness Bob Paisley was brilliant, but he could not always communicate with the players. Joe Fagan had technical knowledge and could communicate but he got the job when, maybe, he was too old for it. Jock had everything. He had the knowledge; he had that nasty bit that managers must have; and he could communicate. On top of that he was six feet tall, and at times he seemed to get bigger when he was talking to you. He had everything that a good manager needs. Nothing ever went by him. He was the best.

Ernie Walker If Jock had lived he would still have been with the Association. Perhaps he would have had a younger manager but we would still have had the job for him. He would never have left us. I told him that. He was important to the Association and I valued his insights. There would always have been a place for him in our set-up.

Jimmy Reid I was at the game in Cardiff, but I didn't see the incident when Jock collapsed. On coming out of the ground I found out he had been taken ill. Hundreds and hundreds of fans were standing outside the ground at the main entrance in a kind of silent vigil waiting for news of how he was. Then a Rangers supporter I know, James Mortimer, came out and told me: 'He's dead.' He was weeping, and I think all of us were. It's difficult to describe your feelings that night.

I went back with Hugh McIlvanney to his hotel in Newport. The bar was filled with Scottish supporters, and in the middle of this a man got up on a chair and made a most moving tribute. He had probably never done anything like that in his life before, but he just seemed to speak for everyone. He said: 'We have lost our manager – but we have lost more than just a manager. We have lost a great man, and a man who brought decency into the game.' He brought silence to the whole place. I doubt if that could have happened for any other man. The grief was widespread.

John Gartland, son of Jock's daughter Ray, the eldest of his grandchildren, who was close to his grandfather.

John Gartland He wasn't like an ordinary grandfather, he was more of a friend, more of a close friend than anything else to me. You could always speak to him and tell him things and he would understand.

He gave you presents and he gave you his love, but there was always something he kept hidden. Hidden from everyone. Something that only he knew, and he kept it away from Nana, and my mum and uncle George and everybody. He would not tell anybody. There was always something he wouldn't share. He spoiled me a lot; too much. I didn't really understand that he was the Scotland manager when the World Cup was on in Spain. Only after that did I begin to realise who he was.

He used to kick a ball about with me in the garden, but he would never try to coach me. He would never be saying: 'You should be doing this', or, 'You should be doing that.' I don't know why. He just left me to pick things up myself.

I miss him every day. Every day that passes he still seems to be with me. When I'm not thinking about anything, I find myself thinking about him.

He never had the chance to see Jonathan, but Stefanie and I have so many memories to share with him when he is old enough to understand. We were lucky to have time with him.

We were watching the game, and Scotland scored, and we all thought that was it. I was sitting with my scarf and my flag. I noticed he didn't jump off the bench, but I thought he was just tense. I didn't know until afterwards that he was dead. It was so hard to understand. Why did it have to be him?

Unknown Scottish supporter on television after the game We'll probably qualify for Mexico now, but I think we would rather miss out on the World Cup if we could have Big Jock back.

Index